"Clear, direct, instructive, we

Cynthia Barlow, *Four Fria*
Death, and L

"From finding your purpose to structuring your experiences, this book will help you share the story that only you can tell."

Anne Janzer, *Get the Word Out: Write a Book That Makes a Difference*

"Boni Wagner-Stafford's simple, succinct manual will get you thinking and moving in your writing. *The Best Memoir* will help you see your work more objectively— anticipating the feedback of any good editor—and steer you away from the bigger mistakes that can set you back in your process, so you can reach your big, final goal of a completed, publishable manuscript."

David R. Morris, Hyponymous Consulting

"A great resource for anyone who wants to write their memoir."

C.A. Gibbs, *The Picture Wall: One Woman's Story of. Being His Her Their Mother*

THE BEST MEMOIR

How to Write It When You Don't Know How

BONI WAGNER-STAFFORD

INGENIUM BOOKS

ISBNs

Paperback: 978-1-989059-67-8

eBook: 978-1-989059-68-5

Audiobook: 978-1-989059-69-2

Contents

Introduction

*M*emoir is about truth. Our personal truth. Not capital T truth, because perception of past events is always filtered through the stained glass windows of our coping mechanisms.

Writing our truth requires bucketloads of courage. Because we must face our fallibility, our flaws, our defects, our culpability. In fact we must do so much more than face these things: we must put them on display for the world to see, like leaping stark naked onto a nudist beach after a lifetime of shame around body image.

The very act (or series of painful, daily acts) of writing requires us to have the courage to stare down the *facts* of our past, to make sense of them, and to show the reader that we've come through it all somehow better, wiser, more resilient—rarely do we aim to leave the reader feeling hopeless because we authors come out the other side of our memoir-writing exercise beaten and bloodied.

Writing memoir is not for the faint of heart.

We write about our past and our lives and in doing so we discover the meaning behind it all. Sometimes, not often, we discover the meaning first, and then decide to write. It's one of the gifts of this process, like giving birth after a long, no-drugs-allowed labour: the self-discovery of what it's all been for.

While the results of our work writing memoir might leave us healed and better able to forge a future, like the ugly duckling transforming into a swan, the sacred part of this journey is actually the relationship we build with the reader. And that requires an emotional transparency and vulnerability we rarely share, if ever, even with those with whom we share our bed.

While I hold the writing of memoir in sacred esteem, there are myriad other issues and moving parts that, as indie authors, it is helpful to be aware of.

what you'll learn in *the best memoir*

You'll learn about the foundational pieces—some business-related, some process, some legal—that it is helpful to have a grasp of before you get too far into the writing process. One of the tools I've used while working with more than two dozen authors is to build this foundation of understanding and knowledge, demystifying the big, exciting, and often overwhelming world of publishing nonfiction.

And that's what we're tackling together first in this book.

You'll learn more about memoir as a sub-genre of nonfiction. You'll see how you fit into this world of published authors and that you do, indeed, fit. You'll get a better sense of where your book idea would fall in the marketplace. You'll learn the basics and myths of copyright so you stay out of trouble. You'll learn about your writing style and how to avoid common traps.

You'll learn how to plan, structure, and create an outline for your memoir. You'll learn about the difference between your truth and the *capital T truth,* and which one is most important to write about. You'll learn about the power of self-awareness, the willingness to be vulnerable, and why you need hefty stores of each. And you'll learn about the roles that perspective and pain play in crafting a great book.

You'll also learn the sharpen-your-pencil elements of craft that will help your reader more clearly *see* what you're saying: point of view, active and passive voice and when each is most appropriate, how to show versus tell, tips for writing better dialogue, and why it's best to strive for plain language.

And finally, you'll learn to identify what kind of writer you are, and how to keep yourself motivated by keeping your eye on the prize.

There is truly so much to learn and to do, so many decisions to make as you embark on the journey of writing and publishing your memoir, that it can be overwhelming. But I promise you: the toughest, most important part is what I've discussed already. The gumption, guts, and sheer bloody-mindedness needed to bring your most vulnerable, self-reflective self to the writing process. Strip away everything else first, and I predict this will fuel the passion you need to get you through the rest. All the techno-babble and publishing hoopla can be learned by anyone: no one but you can write your own masterful memoir and leave your reader in a puddle on the floor. That must be your first, primary, and most important aim.

Let's get started.

FOUNDATIONS FIRST

When building a house, you don't paint the rooms and hang the artwork until the framing and drywall is done. The same concept applies in our writing: understanding these foundational elements will result in a more informed author and a much better book.

1

What's Your Why?

*B*efore you embark on your writing journey, you need to know why you want to go in the first place. And why a reader would want to buy and read your book.

start at the beginning

Your *why* provides the foundation for every decision you make through the process of writing, publishing, and marketing your memoir. It affects everything.

It's why we spend so much time on each and every one of our discovery calls speaking to aspiring authors before we agree to take them on board: we want to know what's motivating them to write and what they believe about why a reader will want their book. It gets them thinking, and through the conversation we learn a lot about the subtler dynamics between us and whether we're a fit for the long, in-depth, and often intimate process that comes with partnering on a book project.

On this it doesn't matter whether you're writing business or self-help or memoir or true crime. The *why* is simply the most important starting point for any book.

let's start with you

Being clear on why you want to write and publish your memoir and to become a published author helps you articulate your aspirations, goals, and objectives for a passion project that no one ever disputes is going to be a lot of work.

Your list of *why* statements becomes the pillar for everything you plan and do related to your book: how you write it, what you include and exclude, design and publishing decisions, marketing and promotion decisions.

Is your objective to:

- Generate income to support yourself and make a decent living with your writing?
- Publish a book that helps grow influence through your business?
- Help others by revealing a poignant personal experience with some lessons?
- Create a legacy of knowledge for family, including future generations?
- Gain credibility before a career change?

In *One Million Readers: The Definitive Guide to a Nonfiction Book Marketing Strategy That Saves Time, Money, and Sells More Books,*[1] we take a deeper dive into the *why* notion, framed as objectives, related to what you want to achieve with your book marketing. I'm going to share an excerpt for you here because it's helpful to see this when you're at the beginning of your book journey.

As you explore all the reasons why you want to write and publish your book, consider all angles: you the person, you the professional, you the author, you the business owner, and your reader. And then, think about the why for each of these categories: awareness, engagement, and sales.

Awareness: What kind of awareness do you want to raise? Is it for you as an author? For your book, or for the subject you're writing about? All of the above? Who is it that needs to be more aware? Is this awareness a prerequisite to change you are advocating?

Engagement: Do you want to speak at conferences and events? Do you want to engage with readers by doing book readings or signings? Do you want to speak at schools, libraries, or business meetings? Do you want to build an online community of loyal readers, or build an engaged email list of readers who will want to buy your next book, and the one after that?

Book sales: How many books do you want to sell? Be realistic and also bold in your answer to this one. Don't say two, but also probably don't say two million. How do you know what's a realistic goal? It depends on the genre; it depends on the marketing strategy; it depends on the quality; it depends on your marketing budget; and it depends on whether you have a team or you're marketing your book solo.

your reader, your audience

Why will your book be desired by and of value to your reader?

What is it you want your reader to know?

What does your reader need from you and your book?

What do you hope to make them think or feel or do once they've read your book?

Do you want to inspire or guide your reader?

what you will do with your why

Knowing the why for you and your reader is going to inform what you're going to write, what kind of language to use, what anecdotes to include (ones that resonate with your reader).

the vacation example

The most basic example of how knowing your why drives the rest of your decision making is the vacation.

Imagine you're planning a vacation. Of course, you're going to think about it in advance. Maybe only a day or two in advance if you're a really spontaneous kind of person, but there has to be a decision to go before you go.

You're going to consider what experience you want on your vacation: are you a thrill seeker looking for an adventure vacation, or do you need two weeks of total downtime on the beach with a stack of escapist books?

Which of those two options feeds your *why* for taking the vacation in the first place is going to influence the destination, your mode of travel, how much money you're going to invest in getting there, the activities that you plan in advance, and what you choose to do when you get there.

If you're a thrill seeker, you might want to hitchhike or take the train. If you really just need two weeks of downtime on the beach, you're going to fly first class. You get the picture. Yup, I'm ready for a vacation too!

So it's the same kind of thing when you're thinking about your why and your goals and your objectives for your nonfiction book. It really helps you target what your path to publishing will look like in a way that has a much better chance of getting you what you want.

be ready for your why to shift

The why you connect with as you start writing your memoir may not end up being the same why when you're done. It may, and often does, evolve over time. It might start broad and become more specific. Or, it might stay the same. Regardless, it's important to have a starting place, and be open for new avenues.

> My 'why' started as just wanting other mothers of transgender adult children to find solace in reading about my experience with the coming out of my eldest child. Through the writing of my story, my 'why' expanded into a larger motherhood message and I also wanted my story to be a resource for all mothers: mothers of autistic, mothers of mentally ill, as well as LGBTQ parents, and not just trans. My journey has taken me to a different place than I expected it to at the beginning.
>
> C.A. Gibbs, author *The Picture Wall: One Woman's Story of Being (His) (Her) Their Mother*

what if you start writing before knowing why?

I never want to say there's a problem when you get down to business and start writing. Just be aware there are implications.

It will affect what you include in your story, how you frame it, and the tone of voice you adopt.

Your *why*, and your goals and objectives, will help you decide which of the things in the publishing process you can keep doing for yourself, and what tasks or functions you would like to hand over to a publishing professional. Do I want to write the first draft myself, or am I going to be better served to start working with a ghostwriter? What type of editor do I need to invest in and work with? What level of design specialists do I need to engage?

And the final thing, perhaps the most important thing about determining your *why*, is the hard wiring that happens with your motivation. Writing and publishing a book is a big, long, and complex project that takes time and energy and focus. And the more you can connect to your *why*, the easier you're making it for the energy to flow to carry you through the long haul.

It is going to make your entire process more effective and efficient.

2

What's Holding You Back?

*W*riter Joseph Epstein is credited with saying, "Eighty-one percent of Americans feel that they have a book in them—and should write it."[1] Epstein's statement was based on a survey, possibly conducted while in his role as instructor at Northwestern University. At the time, back in about 2002, Epstein said this 81 percent represented approximately 200 million people. If the percentage holds true, based on 2020 population levels, the number of Americans who want to write a book is somewhere closer to 260 million.

You may have seen other internet stats, and by that I mean those unattributed and perhaps baseless, that while 81 percent of Americans want to write a book, fewer than 3 percent, or 2 percent, ever do.

So why do so many people want to write a book? It's because human beings are storytellers.

In a 2017 study published in Nature Communications,[2] PhD candidate Daniel Smith argues that far from being a time and energy waster, storytelling plays a key role in knowledge dissemination that helps articulate social norms, organize social behaviour, and encourage cooperation.

Storytelling helps us share the rules of the game. Story is how we have, not just for generations, but for millennia, adapted and evolved.

So: you're helping the human race evolve while you're binge-watching *Outlander* (or whatever else you're watching) on Netflix.

Your *desire* to write a memoir is likely wired into your DNA. Whether it's about a business event, an element of your family history, or a poignant personal experience that will help others, it is part of this vast web of life-giving, life-saving, and species-evolving process. In other words, you're in good company.

Still, desire doesn't fill the page.

limiting beliefs

Might you have limiting beliefs that are holding you back from starting, writing, finishing, and publishing your memoir?

Sometimes false or limiting beliefs are born out of a specific experience. Usually negative.

Here's one of mine.

I could write my name at age three, recite and write the alphabet by age four, and was an early and voracious reader. I loved stories. I loved *Nancy Drew* and the *Hardy Boys* and the *My Book House* books and *Winnie-the-Pooh*. I was in grade four when I read a 500-page book on the history of music. Yeah, I was a real word nerd.

In grade five, my teacher assigned our class an exciting project: write a story with characters and action and I don't now recall what else. But I knew I was going to ace this assignment and even before the teacher finished explaining the details of the assignment my brain was off crafting the plot.

I had so much fun. I decided to use the existing *Nancy Drew* characters and created a brand new mystery story. I did my own research, reverse engineered the solving of the puzzle, and polished my ten-year-old prose until I felt it sang.

Presentation day arrived, and my arm shot up like a geyser when the teacher asked for volunteers to read their assignment in front of the class. Up to the front I went. My story was good. I knew it.

After reading aloud and getting the appropriate applause from my classmates, I placed my written story on my teacher's desk.

When I got the marks back from the teacher, I received a failing grade.

What?

Yup, I failed.

The story was good, said the teacher, the writing showed promise, said the teacher, but she could not give me a passing mark.

Why?

I did not create my *own* characters. My active brain was off and running before she had finished explaining the assignment, and I missed the part where she told the class to be sure *every part of the story was original, including the characters.*

I was devastated.

I lost confidence in my ability. I became nervous about sharing my writing with anyone. This one negative experience lay the foundation of a false belief that would get in my way for decades to come.

I loved writing, and reading, and thinking about writing, but it was clear I could not actually write. I and my grade five teacher had proven that.

Still, I was unable to swim against the tide of my deepest desires.

I joined the yearbook club in high school but shied away from taking on any writing assignments. I looked for a career that would keep me close to writing without requiring that I be a *writer.*

what is a belief?

A belief is just a thought you continue to think. The more you think those thoughts, the more energy the negative belief has, the more energy the negative belief, the more you think the thought. It's a vicious cycle.

Your limiting beliefs tell you writing a good book is impossible and so it is.

Your limiting beliefs tell you that all the good books have been written already, and so you always see a book that's similar to your book idea as a reinforcement that your idea has no merit.

Your limiting beliefs tell you writing a book is hard or even impossible and it is–*for you*.

That's why it's so important to identify your limiting beliefs, so you can eradicate them once and for all.

Want to change a limiting belief? Change the thought. It really is that simple. It's not always easy.

Perhaps you are aware of limiting beliefs you possess with respect to becoming a published author, or reaching the next level of success as an author, though I might guess it's more likely you're unaware.

Here is an exercise that can help you identify those pesky beliefs and begin to cast off the heavy chains holding you back from your desires.

emotions as signposts

Your negative emotions are ready-made signposts for your limiting beliefs. Your thoughts—which you can control—create the emotions you feel as well as being responsible for limiting beliefs. The thought might be fleeting, such that you hardly notice it's been there, but the *feeling* might sweep you away in a disempowering tsunami of internal muck and debris.

Notice what you're feeling at any given time, specifically when you think about writing your memoir. Are you afraid, anxious, restless, impatient, irritable, obsessing, doubtful?

Those are clear signs that whatever you're thinking as you feel those emotions is generating or has generated a limiting belief.

link your feelings with thoughts

Here's an exercise to help you identify and make connections between your feelings and their originating thoughts.

1. make a list of the negative emotions
2. identify the thought that is creating that emotion
3. write that thought down.

I'll demonstrate with a completed exercise.

Fear: I'm afraid I'll never be able to do this.
Anxiety: I'm going to make way too many mistakes.
Embarrassment: People are going to laugh at me, and they'll know I'm a failure.
Discouraged: I've tried things before, and they didn't go well.

rebuttal

This next step is critical if you want to remove your own barriers (your limiting beliefs) to doing and becoming what and who you want. The *doing* is to write and publish your memoir, the *becoming* is the bigger thing, which is an identity change to published author.

Take your list of emotions and the triggering thoughts you've identified in the exercise above, and write the rebuttal: what you know is true.

Building on our example from above:

I'm afraid I'll never be able to do this.

Not true, I have been successful in many of the things I have tried.

I'm going to make way too many mistakes.

Everybody makes mistakes, and I will too. But I can hire someone to proof the draft.

People are going to laugh at me, and they'll know I'm a failure.

First, I'm not a failure. I'm brave for putting myself out there in pursuit of my goals, and I have plenty of examples of things I've accomplished. Second, what other people think is none of my business.

I've tried things before, and they haven't gone well.

That's true, but I have also tried things that have gone well, and I am proud of that.

real life author example

In the event you're still not seeing how this emotion-thought-rebuttal exercise would apply specifically to your memoir-writing endeavour, here is a real-life example from Yvonne Caputo as we were working together developing her manuscript for *Flying with Dad*.

 When you sent me the first edited chapters and I saw all of those red lines, I was embarrassed and ashamed. I was keenly aware of the feeling, but I had to really think, *what was I thinking?* It took me a while to get to the thoughts. I discovered that the thought I had been unaware of was that I was a lousy writer, and I wondered if you thought I was stupid.

Now, those thoughts are untrue, but until I was aware of them I couldn't challenge and say to myself, *Ease up kiddo, you wrote and rewrote a manuscript,*

and you are anything but stupid. You know you've always been a great student.

Yvonne K. Caputo, psychotherapist and author, *Flying with Dad: A Daughter. A Father. And the Hidden Gifts in His Stories from World War II.*

free-writing exercise

On the topic of your desire to write and publish your memoir, start writing down all thoughts that pop into your head. Don't filter, don't edit, don't dismiss anything that pops into your head.

Here are some prompts to get you started:

- What will happen once your book is published? What will you lose? What will you need to change? What might go wrong?
- What is *beyond your control* that is keeping you from writing and publishing your book?
- In what areas are you not good enough to achieve this desired outcome?
- What is it about writing and publishing a book that you *don't want?* Is there something in here you're trying to avoid?
- Why can't you write and publish a book?
- What makes being a published nonfiction author wrong?
- Why don't you deserve to be a published author?

Using these prompts, and whatever else comes into your mind, write until you have absolutely nothing left. You'll know when you're done because your mind will be more calm.

Now, review everything you've written. Underline or highlight, in your favourite colour (I've developed a fascination for everything pink), every negative thought, every idea that is not aligned with your desired outcome of writing, finishing, and publishing a book.

If you're like most people, you will be surprised at some of the things that have spilled out of you.

Everything you've highlighted is a limiting belief. And those are the thoughts to eradicate and replace with something affirmative.

For example, perhaps you wrote, "I don't have time to write every day." Replace that thought with something like, "I've got thirty minutes before breakfast every day and two hours before lunch on Saturdays to focus on my writing."

the author you want to be

It's all about deciding who you are, who you want to be, and how you are going to clear away the wreckage of your negative and limiting beliefs to help you get what and where you want. All the how-to writing tips in the world aren't going to help you if you don't *believe* you have what it takes to write and finish your book.

It's also about seeing yourself as you will be once you finish the book.

Are you an author? Or will you let yourself disappear into the fog as one of the millions of people who want to be an author?

3

What is Memoir

*M*emoir is a sub-genre of nonfiction. Duh. I'm sure you knew that. Someone recently asked me this question, which surprised me, and made me realize this was not a good time to make an assumption. (Is it ever?)

And now I'm going to break another rule of journalistic writing: I'm going to ignore the inverted pyramid formula (that's where all the essential material goes at the top, with the least important material at the bottom) and start with the foundation. Which means that before I get to talking about what memoir is, I'm going to talk about nonfiction.

what is nonfiction?

Nonfiction (according to most of the style guides in British English), rather obviously, is not fiction. The word *fiction* originates from the Latin word *fictionem,* which is a fashioning or feigning.[1] Given that fiction is formed in the imagination, as are the roots of fable, myth, or legend, this makes sense. Fiction can also be used to describe deliberate untruths. Lies. Fantasies.

Nonfiction is the opposite. It's based on fact, truth, and real life. Stories about things that really happened. Imagination may play a role in how facts are packaged, ordered, and framed, as well as in how we derive meaning from those facts, but it is still based on fact.

story

Factual and truthful books, even the most straight-forward and dry academic books, are still *story* at their root. Story is the foundation of everything. Your anecdotes, accounts, perceptions, even how-to steps for others: all of them comprise story. You want to ensure you bow down to the gods of story whether you're writing a business, true crime, self-help book—or a memoir.

so... what is memoir?

Memoir, not surprisingly, comes from the latin word *memoria*[2] and is often seen spelled (incorrectly in Canadian, British, and American English) the French way as *memoire*.

While memoir and biography and autobiography are all closely related, they are different, as follows:

- Memoir is a story based on a particular time period, event, or experience, rather than a complete retelling of the story of one's entire life. Two examples from Ingenium Books' authors are *Four Fridays with Christina* by Cynthia Barlow, and *The Picture Wall* by C.A. Gibbs.
- Biography is written about the entirety of someone else's life: often the subject is a notable figure, celebrity, or politician, written by a third party. An example is the late Canadian journalist and my ex-father-in-law John Gray's 2003 biography of Paul Martin, a former Canadian finance minister, *Paul Martin: The Power of*

Ambition. More recent examples include Mary L. Trump's biography of her uncle, US President Donald Trump, or Jonathan Alter's biography of Jimmy Carter.

- Autobiography, on the other hand, is a first-hand account of the author's entire life: Jimmy Carter's own *A Full Life,* or Woody Allen's *Apropos of Nothing* are two examples.

Using my fifth-grade writing assignment story as an example:

- A *memoir* would use that humiliating event as the central theme, with all elements of the book related to dismantling my limiting self-belief and redefining myself as a writer.
- A *biography* would be written by someone else about my entire life, with my fifth-grade teacher's dressing down after the failed writing assignment as one of many included life events.
- An *autobiography* is like the biography above, only written by me about me. It's a full story of my life, from the beginning to present day, including the failed fifth grade writing assignment.

how memoir fits with other types of nonfiction

When we're talking about trade or general adult nonfiction, which we are, meaning we are excluding academic works and textbooks, there are three main types of nonfiction writing and many more sub-genres. You want to understand this before you begin or get too far into your writing process.

Understanding the other types of nonfiction and the range of sub-genres, or categories, will help you see where memoir fits into the bigger picture of the nonfiction options open to today's reader. You'll also build confidence and credibility because you'll know how your writing style, tone, cover design, and book description deliver what the reader expects from a book they find listed in your category.

(Confused about why we sometimes say genre/sub-genre versus categories? Join the club. The publishing industry talks about genre/sub-genre, while Amazon, the online retailing search engine behemoth, talks about categories. It's the same thing.)

I'm going to describe for you the types of nonfiction in a big picture way and then share a list of sub-genres, or categories, which reveal the way a reader might search for your book on retail sites and in stores.

narrative nonfiction

Narrative nonfiction is simply a way to refer to a particular kind of storytelling. Memoir, autobiography, and journalistic nonfiction (including investigative works like true crime) can all be considered narrative nonfiction. From the reader's perspective, narrative nonfiction delivers an experience closest to fiction: a narrative nonfiction author is taking the reader on a journey. While the reader is learning while reading your narrative nonfiction book, they may not be consciously setting out to learn how to do something.

prescriptive nonfiction

Prescriptive nonfiction is *how-to* nonfiction. Here you focus on explaining your topic and how the reader might apply what you're teaching. Textbooks, self-help books, and how-to books can all be considered prescriptive.

persuasive nonfiction

This type of nonfiction writing is when you're stating your opinion with the aim of influencing your reader to come around to your way of thinking. Books that present a political point of view, advocate for a new approach or policy, or highlight proposed fixes to social inequities would be considered persuasive nonfiction.

categories of nonfiction

The categories that retailers use to help readers find what they're looking for is a more important issue than you might think at first glance.

Imagine you stand in line at your favourite donut shop, finally getting to the front of the queue and you order your favourite: the freshly-baked frosted cinnamon roll that you've been smelling since you opened the door to the shop twenty minutes ago. You pay the cashier and he hands you a still-warm container with your yummy treat inside.

Imagine that when you get back to your car and open the container, instead of a buttery cinnamon roll, you discover a gooey mound of….liver and onions! Yuck! Even if you like liver and onions, it's not what you were expecting. I'd bet you'd be just a little bit upset—maybe a lot upset. You'd march back inside (unless you were already on the freeway) and demand either a refund or an exchange, and you might even leave a nasty review of the business online.

This is the same experience your readers will have if your book ends up in the wrong category: if they're expecting a memoir and you give them a practical play-by-play on how to tie-dye T-shirts, or if they're expecting a book about leadership principles and instead you give them a book of recipes. We don't want that for the readers of our memoir.

So, back to the categories. Here are the main nonfiction book categories:

- Art and Photography
- Autobiography/Memoir

- Biography
- Business and Money
- Cookery
- Crafts, Hobbies and Home
- Education and Teaching
- Families and Relationships
- Health and Fitness
- History
- Humour and Entertainment
- Law and Criminology
- Motivation and Inspirational
- Politics and Social Sciences
- Religion and Spirituality
- Self-Help/Personal Development
- Travel
- True Crime

Most nonfiction books will find a home in more than one category: a book about your experience getting robbed at gunpoint might fit in the autobiography/memoir category as well as law and criminology, and perhaps also, depending on what you've done with the experience, motivational and inspirational.

best-selling nonfiction categories

Most of us want to write and publish a book to sell it. We might dream of becoming a best-selling author who rakes in millions. Yeah. Well, while that is possible, it is not the norm and today it is more difficult than ever with self-publishing serving to proliferate the number of available books (many of them awful quality that harm the reputations of every indie author). A crowded marketplace makes it more important to develop this base understanding about the nonfiction marketplace so we can get clearer on what we need to do to accomplish our goals related to our books.

One of those pieces of knowledge is to know which categories of nonfiction tend to sell better. This is a shifting benchmark, obviously, as trends like current events and technological advancement influence what readers are interested in.

Complicating matters further is the fact that the same book published in a variety of formats, like eBook, paperback, hardcover, and audiobook, will see different ranking results per format. So when you search for *bestselling categories of nonfiction* be prepared to find results that differ between, for example, the hardcover and eBook version. This speaks to reader preference: the reader who prefers to purchase and read a hardcover book is different from the reader who prefers to purchase and read on their digital eBook reader.

So, at the time of this writing, the five best-selling categories for physical paperback books on Amazon are:

1. Memoir and Biography
2. Self Help
3. Religion and Spirituality
4. Health, Fitness, and Dieting
5. Politics and Social Sciences

The five best-selling categories for eBooks on Amazon, on the other hand, are:

1. Religion and Spirituality
2. Biography and Memoir
3. Business and Money
4. Self Help
5. Cookbooks, Food, and Wine

Now you've got a good handle on what memoir is and how it differs from biography and autobiography. You also have a better picture of the broader nonfiction landscape, and why the categories that readers expect to find their books in are so crucial both to exposure and laying the groundwork for a positive reader experience.

Let's talk more now about the reader.

4

Your Reader and Why They Buy

*I*t may sound counterintuitive, but if you write your book believing you're trying to reach everyone, you'll actually reach no one. Try to please everyone, you won't please anyone.

Your reader, in marketing parlance, is your target audience. At least, it's part of your target audience. For most sub-genres of nonfiction, your target audience will also include influencers: the people or organizations that can help you reach more readers. I've written about this in more detail in *One Million Readers: The Essential Guide to a Book Marketing Plan so You Can Save Time, Money, and Sell More Books.*[1]

For your book marketing strategy and follow-on tactics, you'll want to think more broadly and include influencers.

But for the purposes of *writing* your book, your reader is the person you've written your book for. And you want to get to know them well before you even start writing.

Your reader is a person you can name and describe who will benefit from your book and its solutions to their biggest problems.

Your task here is two-fold: build a profile of your target reader, and be sure you have an answer to their big question, which I'll get to in a moment.

your reader profile

Here are the elements you'll want to assemble to create your reader avatar, sometimes called a persona.

- Gender
- Age
- Where they live
- Ethnicity
- Education level
- Interests
- Hobbies
- Passions
- Personality type
- Income level
- Industry and job
- What do they read (blogs/magazines/news sources/books)
- Where do they access this reading material?
- Where are they online? What websites do they visit?
- What social media platforms are they active on?
- What social media networks do they refuse to use, if any?

Now we need to dig a little deeper into the fabric of your reader. What do they want? Is it to earn more money? If yes, why? The reason this is such an important question to answer correctly, to get you to the right reader profile, is that there are a variety of possible answers as to why someone might want to earn more money, and each reason reveals a different core motivation. Is that motivation to have the freedom to travel more, or to pay for a loved one's expensive medical bills, or put their kids through university? These are the types of things I want you to think about as you're answering the next set of questions. And, of course, you want to keep your thought process tied to the topic or genre of your book.

- What is it that frustrates or annoys your reader on a daily basis? (If you're writing a book in the personal finance category, are they tired of running out of grocery money before the end of the month? If you're writing a book for entrepreneurs, are they fed up with what feels like a hamster wheel of busy work but their client list isn't growing? If you're writing a memoir, you'll want to tie one of the big content themes to a daily frustration for your reader.)
- What is your reader afraid of? (Losing the house? The marriage?)
- What does your reader want, more than anything?
- What are your reader's hopes and dreams for the future?

And now, the most important question of all. Imagine your reader asking you, "Out of the hundreds of other books available on this topic, why should I choose your book to read? In fact, why should I buy a book about the topic at all?"

It may be unlikely any reader is actually going to physically stand in front you and ask that question. It is 100 percent certain that this question is the one driving them to purchase, or pass on, your book when they see it for sale.

Think about how you'd answer the reader standing in front of you and write it down: What are the key problems or pain points you have that me and my book can help solve?

You might think this process is easier for the author of another nonfiction sub-genre than it is for you. It's not. Or maybe it is, but whether you're writing memoir or business or self-help, this is the work that will get you closer to the goals than almost anything else you do.

why they buy

It can be helpful at this point to consider what is relatively well known in the world of copywriting, which is why people buy. Anything.

Let's borrow a concept from the world of copywriting, which you'll be well advised to brush up on as this is a key skill needed as soon as you start to market, promote, and sell your book.

What is copywriting? It is the art of persuading someone to do something you want them to do. This might be to click a link, leave their email address, make a purchase, or buy your book.

I was recently reading *Copywriting Secrets* by Jim Edwards.[2] It was the ten reasons why people buy—anything—that caught my eye. Wouldn't that be helpful for authors of nonfiction to know, so they can be clearer about the motivations of their specific reader audience?

At first I thought this would only apply to our audience of nonfiction authors, and not so much to those who write fiction. then I thought again. Fiction, nonfiction, books or widgets, here are the top ten reasons why people buy.

1. To make money
2. To save money
3. To save time
4. To avoid effort
5. To escape mental or physical pain
6. To get more comfort
7. To achieve or attain better health
8. To gain praise
9. To feel more loved
10. To increase popularity or social status.

Understanding these reasons why people buy before you start writing will help you craft a message that clearly delivers on one or more of these areas. And when it comes time to write your book description—that's the sales copy that should be designed to, ahem, encourage the reader to buy—you'll be set to go.

Here's an exercise for you. With your book idea or your manuscript in mind, really push yourself to come up with five to ten different answers to the following questions.

1. How will my book help them make money? (Stretch here on this one: even if your book is a memoir, perhaps one of your answers will be something like, "the reader will feel so inspired and hopeful after reading my book that they'll go to work, perform their jobs better than ever, and get a raise.")

2. How can reading my book help them save money over the next week, month, or year? (Even if it is only that they'll be so busy reading the book they won't be buying expensive coffees at Starbucks, start here.)

3. How much time will reading my book save them?

4. What will they not have to do anymore once they get and read my book?

5. What physical pain does my book eliminate for them and what does that mean for their life and business?

6. How does my book eliminate mental or emotional pain or worry for them?

7. What are all the ways my book can help them feel more comfortable?

8. How does my book help them achieve greater cleanliness or hygiene?

9. How does my book help them feel healthier and more alive?

10. What are all the ways my book is going to help them be the envy of their friends and feel more loved by their family?

11. How will buying and reading my book make them more popular or increase their social status?

Granted, when I first read these reasons and the follow-up questions, I dismissed them as not being relevant to books. And then realized that one of the more difficult and tricky tasks when we're getting ready to publish a book is—the sales description! Of course, readers are buyers, just like every other buyer. And books are products, just like every other product. Information products, but products nevertheless.

You'll thank yourself later, or at least your publisher will, if you tackle this little exercise at the start of your writing journey, then revisit it before you hand the draft manuscript off to your editor.

5

Copyright

*Y*ou might be asking yourself why you need to worry about copyright before you've even started writing your book. It's true this can be a dry, overwhelming topic for the aspiring author. There's a reason I include it in *The Best Memoir*, and there's a reason I include it in the *Foundations First* section and not later on.

You'll save yourself time, energy, and grief by arming yourself with some awareness of copyright issues before you get too deep into the writing process. You might even save yourself some money on the editing side, because your editor won't have to spend her time pointing out so many copyright no-no's in your work.

Feel free to skim over this chapter, and the next, and then return to it for a review when you're farther along in the writing process. Please do at least skim over it now.

COPYRIGHT IS ONE OF THOSE BREAD-AND-BUTTER ISSUES that I believe more authors need to become better informed about. Copyright can be a tricky subject. But it's important.

The purpose of copyright is to protect your ability to benefit from your work, both economically and otherwise, while at the same time encouraging creativity and fostering the free, but orderly, exchange of ideas.

copyright is property with real value

Copyright is a type of property under copyright law: intellectual property. You can sell, purchase, assign, or include copyright in your will to pass it on to your heirs.

Any type of creative work of an author, whether it is a nonfiction book, poem, helpful pamphlet, or other document, has intrinsic value and may be monetized.

Copyright, at its core, literally means "the right to copy."[1] Today's copyright laws provide creators of a work, including authors of written material, with legal ownership and the exclusive right to reproduce, perform, or publish a work.

Copyright laws exist to protect your intellectual property (IP) rights as a creator. Conversely it also exists to protect the IP rights of the other authors and creators whose works you consult and reference in the course of writing your book. Awareness and an abundance of caution are in order.

Don't let yourself walk into a legal minefield by inappropriately including someone else's copyrighted information in your work. (I'll cover a couple of other legal matters in the next section, *Ready Set Plan*.)

As we were planning and building out our publishing company, Ingenium Books, I wanted to be able to offer our authors (and ourselves) a deeper level of understanding and comfort around copyright. In 2018, I obtained a Certificate in Canadian Copyright Law from Copyright Laws.[2] The courses covered areas including:

- Practical international copyright
- Digital copyright management
- Copyright permissions

- Managing copyright issues
- Legally using images
- and more

The advice I'm passing on to you here are the high-level pieces I think are most important for you to grasp as you begin your author journey.

let's talk copyright myths

It's easy to get lost in the legalese around copyright, to be confused about what copyright really means, and what you, as a creator of intellectual property (that's your writing), have to do in order to be protected by copyright.

Myth: *Copyright protects ideas.*

Ideas are not protected by copyright law. "He stole my idea!" Legally, under copyright law, it is not possible to steal an idea. Ideas are part of the public domain and no one gets to have a monopoly on them. Copyright law protects the expression of ideas rather than the ideas themselves.

Myth: *You have to pay to register and ship physical copies to a copyright register in order for copyright to apply to your work.*

This is false. The moment your words are affixed, whether onto a computer screen like the one I'm writing on right now, or onto paper in some form, copyright applies.

There are certain exceptions on when the copyright owner's authorization is required and when it isn't. We'll get to that in a bit.

There are benefits of registration. A certificate of registration of copyright provides evidence that a copyright exists because it confirms that the registered individual (you) is the copyright owner. However, should you be subject to infringement, the certificate may not make it any easier for you to defend your copyright. It may, however, make it easier for those who wish to seek permission to use your copyrighted work.

Myth: *My work isn't protected unless I use the © symbol.*

Under Canadian copyright law, you're not required to mark your work with the © copyright symbol. You do not need to register your work with the Canadian copyright office in order to use the copyright symbol.

If you do use it, the format is: the symbol ©, followed by the copyright owner's name, and the year of initial publication. It would look like this:

© Tom Earl Jones 2018

In the US, the advice is copyright symbol>year>name, however relating to Canadian copyright law we found the advice above:[3] copyright symbol-name-year.)

While it may not be *necessary* to use the symbol, I don't see any reason why you wouldn't. Let's shout from the treetops that this original work is, indeed, under the protection of copyright.

Myth: *There is a squad of copyright police.*

Not true. It is your responsibility to monitor and take action against those you feel might be infringing on your copyright. On the Canadian Intellectual Property Office (CIPO) website, for example, is the statement that it is "not responsible for policing of checking on registered works and how people use them."[4] CIPO cannot guarantee that your copyright, registered or otherwise, won't ever be challenged, infringed, or questioned.

Myth: *Book titles can be copyrighted.*

No. In general, copyright of written work applies when it is fixed in tangible form, and longer than a single sentence. Since titles are usually short—one, two, or three words—they are not subject to copyright. So that means you can choose a title for your book even if someone else has published another book with the same title, and someone else can choose the same title for their book that you've chosen for yours. No law against that. However, the consideration becomes one of clarity, reader confusion, and marketing. If there's another book with the same title in the category you're planning to publish in, you'll want to ask yourself whether the reader confusion is worth it.

international copyright

Copyright laws vary country by country, but there are international copyright treaties that govern how copyright is applied across borders. After all, we live in a globalized world, where information products in both digital and electronic form are commonly sold across borders.

In 1886, the signing of the Berne Convention in (you guessed it) Berne, Switzerland, for the first time standardized copyright laws around the world. At the time of this writing, 175 signatory countries are part of the Berne Convention for the Protection of Literary and Artistic Works. With a total of 192 countries world-wide, this means that the vast majority of nations around the world respect each other's copyright laws.

The Berne Convention grants *minimum standards of protection.* There might be differences in the standards of copyright protection between signatory countries, but the Berne Convention ensures that all work by nationals of participating states is granted the minimum standards of protection. For creators like you, that includes the following rights:[5]

- The right to translate your work
- The right to make adaptations
- The right to perform in public
- The right to recite in public
- The right to communicate in public
- The right to broadcast
- The right to reproduce the work manner
- The right to use the work in an audiovisual work

These rights are called economic rights. As an author, a creator, you may create and sell digital or physical copies of your book, display your work in public, perform your work in public, and create other work based on your previously created work. When working with international distributors, don't fall for any schemes in which they try to convince you that you need to pay them extra or provide additional approvals before they can distribute your work.

when permission isn't required

There are times when you might not need to approach another creator for permission to use parts of their work, and when others may not need to approach you for permission to use parts of your work.

In the context of international copyright, these exceptions are known as free use:

- Quotations and other short excerpts of a work, *reproduced for teaching*
- Using works related to current events to report in the newspaper and similar formats
- Broadcasting short recordings of your work
- Developing countries can reproduce and translate an author's work without authorization if it is to be used *for teaching purposes*

free use, fair use, fair dealing

Take note that free use, fair use, and fair dealing may sound similar but they aren't interchangeable terms.[6]

'Fair use' and 'fair dealing' are specific respectively to American and Canadian copyright law. The former is more open-ended in fair use interpretation than the latter. If you want to read more about these differences, check out our US copyright article,[7] our Canadian copyright article,[8] our UK copyright article,[9] or our Australia copyright article.[10]

how long copyright lasts

Generally speaking, copyright lasts fifty to seventy years beyond the author's death. The Berne Convention's minimum standard is fifty years, it's fifty years in Canada, while in the US, UK, and Australia, it's seventy years. (There are some cases where copyright can be extended, but I don't want to get into that here.)

Once the copyright term has passed, the work is considered to be public domain, and you or others are free to use it. Not steal it, not plagiarize it, but use it and provide the appropriate reference or citation.

bottom line

You—and you alone—are in control of protecting your work.

We can all appreciate the value of having our own original works protected by copyright. It only makes sense to ensure we do our best to respect the copyright of other creators.

As a responsible author—indie, hybrid, or traditionally published—be aware of your rights and know how to obtain permissions when you wish to use the work of others. That's where we're headed next.

6

Copyright and Permissions

*K*nowing how and when to obtain permission to quote is something that confounds every indie author at some point of their writing career. Perhaps at some point with every book. In your memoir, you may want to include a favourite poem or song lyrics. It makes sense, as we often feel a deep connection between these words and our experiences.

Unless you have a lot of lead time before you want to publish your book and wish to navigate the world of locating agents and publishers and artists' unions as you try to find the right person to ask for permission, it's often not worth the trouble. And even if it is worth the trouble, you might not be happy with the catch accompanying the permission: a fee. Creators in the music industry are well organized around copyright and licensing issues that directly affect their pocketbooks.

It isn't impossible to get permission, of course. I recently read the book *How the Light Gets In* by Canadian author Louise Penny. She included lyrics from a Leonard Cohen song, and in the acknowledgements she noted that the prolific songwriter not only gave her permission but gave it for free. Penny and Cohen were both living in the Montreal area at the time, so they were part of the same creative community. Not every songwriter is like the late

Leonard Cohen, and those in charge of Cohen's intellectual property today are not guaranteed to be as magnanimous toward another author as Cohen was with Penny.

Think about how you'd handle requests that come your way from other authors wishing to use a quote or excerpt from your published work. Are you going to be as magnanimous as Cohen? More strict with how you dole out permission?

permission to quote

When it comes to determining when and when not to quote from another source, there are several factors to consider.

- **Age of the quote.** Is the work already in the public domain (fifty to seventy years after the death of the author, depending on country of origin)? If yes, permission to quote is not required. Some authors, or their estates, will assign copyright to extend beyond these timeframes, so you have to be cautious.
- **Advertising slogan or trademark.** The major exception to the public domain rules: regardless of when they were created, conceived, and fixed, any slogan or trademark still in use remains protected by copyright.
- **Distinctiveness of the quote.** Even if the excerpt you intend to use is quite short, if it is distinctive and well-known, you can't count it safe to use without obtaining permission to quote. A cunningly devised short phrase may actually contain very unique and original expression that is protected. There is no safe minimum standard on how many words you are permitted to quote prior to risking copyright infringement. It depends on the author, the circumstances, the success of your book, and a host of other subjective and

variable issues. A general rule is: the shorter the quote, the better chance you can use it without permission.

facts are fair game

Facts in and of themselves do not fall under the protection of copyright, which protects *original expression.* Historical dates, events, statistics, names and birthdates—are all facts that cannot be copyrighted. I recommend you keep careful track of your sources for the facts you use in your memoir, for a later decision on whether you wish to include bibliography or reference information.

seeking permission to quote

The process of seeking permission involves contacting the copyright owner directly, or their estate, or their agent/publisher, and making a direct request for use of the work. You may have to sign a contract and pay a fee to use the work.

Keep a spreadsheet and track your requests, the responses (or lack thereof) and the results so that if, in future, you are required to show the efforts you undertook to obtain permission to quote, you will easily be able to do so.

7

Choose Your Style Guide

*Y*ou don't have to think about your style guide until after you've written at least your first draft, but I guarantee you it will ease the editing process and cost if you do. Writing in a consistent style right from the start will save you time later on.

how a style guide helps you

You've probably faced at least one of these conundrums (and if you haven't, you will) in your writing: do you write out the number 'twenty-seven' or simply write '27'? Do you hyphenate 'co-operation' or leave out the hyphen as 'cooperation?' 'Single' or "double" quotation marks? When do you use italics and when do you use bold? Do you write book titles in title case, italicized, or in quotation marks? Do you refer to a single person of unknown gender as "he", "she", "s/he", or "they"?

You won't find answers to these issues in a dictionary. You will find them in a style guide.

what is a style guide?

A style guide, sometimes called a manual of style, is a set of principles to help you produce consistent writing. Refer to a style guide to help you decide about issues like hyphenation and punctuation in the same way you'd check a dictionary for the meaning of words. While not a set of grammar rules, a style guide may include recommendations for sentence construction too. Or whether and when to choose passive voice. Some style guides also recommend the type of words that promote inclusivity and help you avoid inadvertent racism, sexism, homophobia, and other forms of discrimination.

There are three levels of style guide from which to choose.

style sheet

The first, and simplest, is a style sheet. This is usually a short list of tips specific to the manuscript you're working on. You can draw this up yourself before you start writing and add to it as you go along. When you send your manuscript to your editor, it's a good idea to include your style sheet so that you're on the same page. (Pun intended!) Your editor may add to the style sheet too and include it when sending the manuscript to a proofreader.

If you're working with a publisher, and you jointly decide a style sheet is appropriate for your memoir, you'll probably develop it together.

style manual

The second type of style guide is a publisher's house style manual. Traditional publishers usually have their own preferences about style, so they create their own house style manuals for their authors, editors, and proofreaders to use during the process of creating a book. When I worked for the Ontario government, I and my team—all ministries in fact—used a government-wide style guide to frame all of our writing. It addressed treatment of numbers, abbreviations, and other stylistic elements. *Per cent* was two words, for example, never *percent*. These house style manuals are a more detailed version of a style sheet.

professional style guide

If you're an indie author, you probably won't be using a publisher's house style manual. However, you may find it of great help to use this third level of style guide: a formal professional style guide or manual of style. It's a comprehensive reference book that covers just about everything you may want to know about writing for a specific industry. You may want to refer to this style guide as you make stylistic decisions relevant to your manuscript.

You don't have to stick religiously to what the style guide says. For example, you may use an American style guide as a general guideline but tweak the rules to adapt to British English, or vice versa.

how to choose your style guide

Choosing a style guide that you're unfamiliar with will slow down your writing and may prove to be frustrating. Instead, consider a style guide suited to the variety of English you're going to use. You'll find that many of the suggestions in the guide will come naturally to you already. To decide which style guide to use, ask yourself these questions:

1. *Am I familiar with the style?*

Each country has general style guides that are more commonly used. For example, popular style guides in the United States include *The Chicago Manual of Style* and *The Elements of Style*, also known as Strunk and White after its authors. For most memoirs written and published for a general adult audience in the US or Canada will be best served using *The Chicago Manual of Style*.

In the United Kingdom, *New Hart's Rules* and Fowler's *Dictio-*

nary of Modern English Usage are two of the most well-known style guides. Canadian authors often refer to *The Canadian Style: A Guide to Writing and Editing*. In Australia, the *Style Manual: For Authors, Editors and Printers* is the one used most often.

2. *Who is my audience?*

Different industries or professions use different style guides too. Book authors normally use the more general style guides. Journalists in the United States may use *The Associated Press Stylebook*, also called AP Style. When I was a journalist in Canada, we followed *The Canadian Press Stylebook*, aka CP Style. That's likely still the case for Canadian journalists today. In the UK, they'll write according to the style guides published by the BBC, The Economist, The Guardian, or The Times.

Other examples of industry-specific style guides include:

- *MLA Handbook* for academic writing in the United States
- *The Bluebook: A Uniform System of Citation* for legal documents in the United States, the *Oxford Standard for Citation of Legal Authorities* for legal documents in the United Kingdom, and the *Canadian Guide to Uniform Legal Citation / Manuel canadien de la référence juridique*–also called The McGill Guide–for legal documents in Canada
- *American Psychological Association Style Guide*, or APA Style, and the *American Sociological Association Style Guide* or ASA Style for the behavioural and social sciences in the United States
- *American Medical Association Manual of Style*, or AMA Style, for medical writing in the United States
- *The ACS Style Guide: A Manual for Authors and Editors* and *The ACS Style Guide: Effective Communication of Scientific Information* for scientific writing in the United States.

You don't have to stick to only one style guide. If you write for a specific industry, you can use a style guide for that industry in conjunction with a more general style guide.

adopt or adapt a style guide?

You can choose to adopt one of the well-known guides, such as *The Chicago Manual of Style* (CMOS), or you can adapt your own by combining elements of one or more guides.

For example: for this book (and most of the books we publish where the author and the main market are in the US) we've selected CMOS. Among other things, CMOS dictates the treatment of numbers, where numbers one through ninety-nine are spelled out and numbers 100 and over are placed as numerals.

While CMOS also recommends title case for all subheads, we have chosen an all lowercase style for our subheads, in part so I could make this very point and in part because we kinda like the friendly, informal tone that helps us set.

The key is that whatever style guide you pick, whether you purposefully set out to break some rules and adhere to others, is that you maintain consistency through your entire book.

Remember that a style guide is exactly what it says it is: a guide rather than hard and fast rules. Still, it will help you with those niggling little things. You'll know how to punctuate your lists, how to write about money, when to capitalize, and more.

Your writing is indeed a matter of style.

READY SET PLAN

The road to the best memoir is paved with self-awareness, pain, vulnerability, and planning. It helps—no, it pays—to be ready.

.

8

Narrative Plot Structure

*E*very story, regardless of genre, is about transformation. Simplified, every story follows this: problem, change, mastery of problem. Or, a character (in your memoir, you) pursues a need, encounters conflict, and eventually prevails over hardship.

Every story. Film, fiction, memoir, children's book. Including yours.

The story you're telling in your memoir changes you in some way, which affects your perception of the world around you.

you can't start without structure

While working for the telephone company in my early twenties, I took broadcast journalism and television arts courses at night. I also started volunteering with a neighbourhood television station. When the producer handed me my first real reporting assignment, I was pumped. An experienced cameraperson helped me do interviews, coached me through my stand-up (where you speak directly into the camera for a portion of the story), and in a whirl we were back in the edit bay ready to put my first-ever television story together.

And I FROZE. I was supposed to *write* it. I had absolutely

NO IDEA how to put all the pieces of the story together. I couldn't remember anything I was learning in my night school courses.

It was like standing at the edge of a cliff. I wanted to do this so badly, but I could not see how to pull this information together into a cohesive story.

I didn't know how to create the structure so that I could get both myself and the viewer from point A to point B. And I had that pesky little self-belief that I couldn't actually write.

Thankfully, the kind producer joined me in that community TV edit bay and with gentle coaching, together we created a story structure and a script. Aha! Things clicked into place. I learned to see the beginning, the middle, and the end. I saw how to write the script to package all these elements—pictures, sound, graphics, me on camera—into a story that would make sense to the people who would watch it.

Soon I was doing more than crafting my own stories: I was leading story workshops at the community TV station; I was producing network-wide multi-show specials and writing the scripts for reporters and crews all over the region to take with them in the field so we could be sure they got what we needed for each story. It hadn't taken that long to get to this point, and I knew this was the field I wanted to work in, not just volunteer in: television.

I was thrilled when I got my first television news job. It didn't matter that I had to move 500 miles north, away from friends and family, to a town where I didn't know a soul. This was my calling! I found myself on another steep learning curve, again learning more and faster the practical application of theoretical concepts my college courses tried to teach. I made some pretty spectacular mistakes, too. But I was reading radio news reports, covering local events for the evening TV news. And writing, writing, writing every day.

As I rose through the ranks, from weekend reporter to Monday-to-Friday reporter, and then to news anchor and talk show host, I also had the opportunity to work on a long-form documentary news project. Making one hour of television on a single subject was a far cry from making a one- or two-minute news story.

Again, I had no idea how to bring all the content pieces together. This time, I had a long-time and award-winning journalist by my side. He showed me how, sitting on the floor of the lunchroom at the station after everyone had gone home, to put each idea on a single recipe card. We spread them all out on the floor and started moving them around. Soon, I saw a structure emerge and was able to write the documentary and supervise the editing process.

My documentary won several awards. My news reporting won several awards. I spent fifteen years working in television, reporting live from the field, as legislature bureau chief for a string of stations, as news anchor, and as talk show and interview host. I'd become so comfortable looking at a jumble of information and seeing story structure emerge that it was very much second nature.

If this is your first memoir, your first book, and you're not in a job where you're writing a new story every single day, you're not likely going to instantly find comfort with the world of story structure the way I have after intensive, daily immersion. But the point I want you to hear is that you cannot begin writing without a structure. Or if you do, what you'll have is a series of diary entries, not a manuscript.

what structure does

Think of the structure of your memoir as that invisible guide, gently taking the hand of your reader as they weave through the labyrinth of the experience you're writing about. They won't know they're being guided, they won't notice your structure, but they won't feel lost while they're reading your story, either.

Your structure is also a somewhat more visible guide for you as you write about where you started, what you've learned, how you've grown and changed, what you know now as a direct result of the ring around a set of experiences that have shaped the person you are today.

choosing your structure

The importance of crafting a structure that supports this journey you've been on—start, challenge/problem, learning, set-back, growth, change—can't be understated. Keep this journey in mind as we move into the discussion below about the potential plot structures you can adopt to support the telling of this journey.

You've likely heard of the three-act structure: beginning, middle, end. There are more complex and sophisticated structures but this is likely the best choice for the new memoir writer. Each of the variations I describe below is still a three-act structure. As you read about them, remember they all have at their core a beginning, middle, and end.

chronology

The most common application of the three-act structure is chronology. You start with the beginning, or the set-up act. You're setting the scene: introducing the protagonist and describing the event that sets the protagonist's story in motion. The middle, or the confrontation act, describes the protagonist's journey and the obstacles and characters they encounter along the way. In the middle, you may also introduce an antagonist. The antagonist doesn't have to be an actual person but can be a major challenge instead: something like societal beliefs, for instance, or a process/thing that needs figuring out. Throughout the confrontation act, you're building up the suspense. Then, finally, you come to the third part, or the resolution act. This is where the protagonist and antagonist face off: the climax that you've been building towards. After the climax, you tie up the loose ends and emphasize what you want your reader to take away from it all.

manipulating time

With this structure, you start your story somewhere in the middle and then use flashbacks to show your reader how it all began. You can also jump forward to future events and then go back to an earlier point in time. This structure is especially effective when there's a risk that your reader may lose interest in the set-up and just wants to know what will happen next.

circular

Here you start your story with the climactic event that would normally come at the end. You then go back to the beginning and then the middle, describing what led to this climactic event. At the end of the book, you reiterate the climactic event and tie up the loose ends.

parallel

With this structure, you're telling two or more story lines at the same time. Each separate story has its own beginning, middle, and end. You can weave the stories together or tell them separately but at the end, be sure to tie them together.

YOU MAY FIND IT EASIEST TO DIVIDE YOUR BOOK INTO sections or chapters according to the logical progression of the central theme of your memoir. Go ahead and tackle each phase of the progression in order, being sure to build an overarching narrative to connect one step or principle to the next.

Still confused about building your structure? Not to worry. It often happens organically, hand-in-hand with creating your outline. And that's where we're headed next.

9

Draft Your Outline

*C*reating an outline is what comes next once you've had a good think about the structure, as discussed in the previous chapter.

If you're a first-time author, this might be where you get stuck. Even if you've written a book before, creating your starting outline can be tricky. You have the big picture idea of the book you want to write, ideas swirl around in your head day and night, but when you try to picture how everything is going to hang together, you can't see it. You can't figure out where to start.

Almost nobody can sit down and write a book starting with chapter one and bang out the next chapters effortlessly, in the final order they'll appear in on publish day, without first having a clear map for the journey.

That map is your outline.

With this outline you'll feel comfortable and enabled to write in chunks, chapters, segments, or anecdote-by-anecdote as inspiration comes, without worrying about what came before or what comes next.

Enter the easy outlining process. I use this process with great success with every author I'm working with—and I use it on my own work.

the random brainstorm

Start by capturing every notion, idea, concept, topic, and even research elements (if there are any related to your memoir) that you think you might want to include. Write them down: make a list, draw on a whiteboard, use sticky notes on a wall, write on index cards, or speak into a voice recorder and use transcription software to put your words into a document. Whatever works for you in a way that lets the ideas flow. Don't worry about the order, don't judge the relevance or perceived lack thereof, don't filter anything out for any reason.

This will unleash your creativity. You'll start to see how the jumble of ideas that's been keeping you awake at night with their crashing sounds can work together to help you achieve your goal: which at the moment is to write the best memoir.

begin grouping

Next begin organizing all your ideas into groups. How you do this will depend on the tool you've used to capture the ideas: if you've used index cards, you can shuffle them around on a large table or the floor, or use push-pins and a big cork board.

You're still not worrying about the order of the ideas, just the lumping together of things that make sense to be together.

Here's how John Newell, author of *Let It Out: Train your voice to be free, free your voice to be trained*,[1] describes his approach to this part of the outlining exercise in a blog post for Ingenium Books: [2]

 Back in university, before I had regular access to a computer, each essay assignment of mine would start as a rough, abbreviated, handwritten bullet list of everything I thought needed to be said, including anything relevant from research.

I then drew matching symbols beside points that belonged together.

For example, the first point I wrote down would get an asterisk next to it. Any other list item that belonged with it also got an asterisk. For the next topic, I'd use a triangle. Then a square. Eventually every bullet point had an asterisk, triangle, square, cross, circle, or star beside it. I had the basis of sections and paragraphs for an assignment. Next I decided what order the groups would go in. Then I numbered the points within the groups.

grouping suggestions for memoir

The grouping suggestions here can be applied to any sub-genre of nonfiction, although they are particularly relevant to memoir.

- Backstory: things that set the stage for the reader to understand how you arrived at the starting point
- Start: thoughts, events, situations which trigger the start of the journey you're depicting in your memoir
- Challenge/problem: where it got hard for you.
- Learnings: the seeds of awareness that you begin to have that things are different, that you need to think/do something differently, that the world is different than you thought or knew before
- Set-back: when we try something new, there is always a set-back, a push-pull of energy that tries to put things back the way they were or have always been
- Growth: more successes at the new way than set-backs
- Change: your response, both internally and externally, beginning to change from how you'd normally respond
- Become: who you are now, different from the way you were at the beginning of the story

If you really want to geek out on these elements, which you may notice form a story arc, narrative arc, and character development arc, do a Google search on the Hero's Journey[3] and read about it. Here's a simplified list of the phases of the Hero's Journey:

1. limited awareness of problem
2. increased awareness
3. resistance to change
4. overcoming resistance
5. committing to change
6. experimenting with first change
7. preparing for big change
8. attempting a big change
9. consequences of first change attempt (steps and setbacks)
10. renewed dedication to change
11. final push to big change
12. mastery of problem

play with the order of your groups

With your ideas and topics all nestled into groups, you may find you can see what the logical order, or structure, is and how you will move from one group to the next in your book. When you're writing memoir, you'll likely find there's more than one way you could think about ordering your groups. But remember, you're still not casting anything in stone.

Regardless, now it's time to organize the topics into an order that seems to make sense within each of your groups.

example from denise collins's memoir

At the time of this writing, I'm working with author Denise Collins on a memoir about losing her husband of thirty-two years to suicide, her grief process, and the shocking things she learned about that likely contributed to his decision to end his life.

We'd already worked together on articulating Denise's goals for her book, and we knew who she wanted to reach. Denise came to us at Ingenium Books after she'd written the first 10,000 words because she got stuck, didn't know where to go next, and knew she wanted this to be the best book possible.

As Denise and I worked together through a version of this brain dump and grouping exercise, three groups of information appeared: the backstory, the event, and grief.

The backstory grouping is about Denise's past, meeting her husband, and stories from their lives together, the ups and the downs.

The event grouping covers everything about the suicide itself: the morning of, the knock on the door from the police, the funeral, and the inquest.

And the grief grouping will cover everything related to Denise's coming to grips with the loss and unexpected life without her husband.

The outline we developed will weave together the backstory and event, so the reader learns more about each character as they learn more about the details surrounding the suicide, including the shocking and violent method Denise's husband chose to end his life, and how this was out of character for him. And the book will wind up with the content around grief.

Writing each of the three groups became easier, because Denise could focus on writing everything in the backstory, everything about the event, and everything about grief that she wanted to say before we start to weave the elements of backstory and event together.

Doing this work gave Denise a clear picture of what the end looks like, propelling her out the other side of the morass of swirling ideas that had her stuck not knowing where to go. She could *see* that she did indeed have a book on her hands, and she could *see* where the idea she was inspired to work on fit within this working structure.

a final check

Before you head off into the sunset writing to your new outline, it'll be wise to hold each topic from your brainstorm up against the light of your purpose, goals, and objectives for the book, and what your ideal reader is going to want, need, and expect. It's likely you've included ideas in your brainstorm that don't necessarily fit the tight trajectory of your memoir: remember that we are talking memoir and not autobiography. Your memoir is about one specific type of memory, experience, or period of time, and not about your whole life. Backstory is important to include when it provides context that is directly related to the main storyline of your memoir. It's extraneous otherwise.

summary of the steps

1. Brainstorm all your ideas, every potential inclusion for your book
2. Group all of your similar/related ideas
3. Within each group, place the ideas into an order that makes sense to you
4. Remember this outline is not set in stone. Its purpose, at this point, is to help you see that you have a book, and to provide a visible link between ideas swirling in your head and where that idea fits—so that you can begin writing and remove writers block
5. Check each topic against your purpose, goals, objectives, and ask whether your reader needs to know this. Save culled topics for your next book

So, get dumping. Take your maelstrom of thoughts and create a gloriously messy list. You'll be ready for happier, more productive writing.

10

Perspectives and Truth

*W*hen writing memoir, you're obviously going to write about what happened. But you want to leave your reader feeling the emotional implication of *what it means.*

This requires you to think, rethink, and repeat, digging deep into what it was about the particular event that you've decided to include that contributes to the meaning, the learning, and how you've changed as a result.

it's your memoir, your truth

There's truth, and then there's capital T truth. Your memoir is about the former, almost never about the latter.

You have a unique viewpoint because of your direct experience. Your perception is your truth. No one else shares exactly the same perception of your experience as you. You know what you've been through, what's happened to you in your life, and it is your reality, your truth.

What does this mean?

Conducting extensive research of scientific or academic studies may reveal conclusions that contradict your perception, *but they do not make it any less relevant or truthful.*

Don't let the research of *facts* derail your belief in your story or the validity and relevance of sharing it with others who will benefit.

That said, I do want you to be discerning about your beliefs, conclusions, and position on the *facts* of the very memories you're writing about.

It's normal practice for authors to ask family and friends to review early drafts of the manuscript and provide feedback. Where these people have participated or witnessed the same event or experience that's the focus of your memoir, it's likely their perspective of the *facts* may differ from yours.

That doesn't make your perspective wrong. Memory is fallible, for everyone. Like the game of broken telephone, ask any two people to describe an event they both witnessed and you will get two different accounts.

Letting how others may have experienced the same events influence how you portray your memories of them will erode your authenticity and weaken your words.

protect your perspective from the light

When iron is exposed to oxygen and water, it will rust. Its outer surface and appearance have changed, because of its exposure. But it did start out as rust-free iron.

Your memories are like that. Time, experience, and exposure can alter what you see in your memory.

Like a beam of white light passing through a prism, you want to write, initially, about that white light, from the point of view of the white light. It's only later, as your story arc develops, that you pull apart the red, orange, blue, green, and violet beams of light that are dispersed out the other side.

As you process and play with the prose around your perspective on a memory, or memories, watch for signs there's been an alteration. Trust how you feel when thinking about those memories, how you remember feeling at the time, and don't rationalize those feelings away or question their validity unless you're writing that into the story.

protecting relationships when writing memoir

There's a difference between staying true to your own perceptions of what you're writing about and protecting the relationships you have with others who were witness to or feature somehow in your memoir.

It's normal to be concerned about backlash from telling your story, especially if it involves anything that might portray others in less than positive light.

> It would be lovely to tell stories that were free of conflict and strife, but that's not usually why we write our stories and it definitely isn't why people read them. Biography and memoir are noble contributions to the human dialogue. We write it to understand ourselves, and we read it to see ourselves in others.
>
> Trina Holt, Ingenium Books contributor

There are a few key questions to ask yourself that will help you stay on the safe side of the relationship fence.

1. Are you writing out of bitterness or revenge? This is not a suitable motivation to write.
2. Can you write about someone's role without imposing your conclusion about what they said or did on the reader? In short, can you let the reader decide?
3. Are you owning up to your own fallibility and being really honest?
4. Do you have to include all the detail that paints

someone in a negative light, or will your story hold just as well without it?

As Trina Holt said, we write memoir to understand ourselves, and we read memoir to see ourselves in others. We don't write memoir to show how horrible other people are. We are all flawed, we all struggle, we are all composed of a little good stuff along with some bad. As long as you're courageous enough to take responsibility for your own actions and beliefs, your writing will have more power.

11

Self-Awareness, Pain, Vulnerability

*H*ow would you rate your level of self-awareness? Your willingness to be vulnerable? To write the best memoir, you need hefty stores of each.

 Our data reveals that 95 percent of people believe they are self-aware, but the real number is 12-15 percent. That means, on a good day, about 80 percent of people are lying about themselves—to themselves.

Tasha Eurich, *Insight: The Surprising Truth About How Others See Us, How We See Ourselves, and Why the Answers Matter More Than We Think.*

self-awareness

You need to be able to open up your beliefs and actions to your own deep and humble scrutiny. Your awareness of the emotional and psychological conflicts raging within feeds the character expression unleashed through your writer's voice. It's you. The real you. In your head, in your heart, on the page: your reader wants and deserves all of you. And she can't get what she deserves if you are unable or unwilling to go there.

Self-awareness is internal and external.[1] The two forms are independent of one another: you can be strong in one without being strong in the other.

Internal self-awareness: knowledge of your strengths, weaknesses, and values.

External self-awareness: knowledge of how you are perceived by others.

You can start to improve your self-awareness by questioning what you think you know about yourself. Answer these questions:

- Who am I?
- Why am I the way I am?
- Why do I react to things as I do?
- Others don't see things the way I do, what about me causes that?
- What motivates me?
- When I feel something strongly, where do I feel it in my body?
- What childhood experience was the first time I felt that strong emotion?

You'll find that as you consider the questions, new thoughts and awareness will continue coming to you even after you complete the exercise. Keep coming back to your answers, and watch how your self-awareness will deepen and grow. Use this new depth in your writing.

pain

We process and categorize our memories to avoid pain. If you want to write the best memoir, it's going to hurt. You experienced the pain the first time around, and you're going to open yourself up to experience it all over again when you write about it.

Pain is uncomfortable and intolerable. It is also the seed from which life grows, the oyster producing the pearls of wisdom we drape around our throat, and a necessary element of every good story.

The stories that are the richest and most helpful to your readers are those where the experience caused the author some level of physical or emotional trauma.

I'm not saying that your memoir needs to be only about pain, but every human journey involves it. Ignore it or leave it out at your peril.

healing from trauma

If your memoir is dealing with severely traumatic events, which many are, you need to be sufficiently healed enough before you start writing. Too soon and you risk writing material that will be too emotionally exhausting for the reader, and that doesn't deliver the benefit of perspective and progress that healing brings—to both life and writing.

 Be careful you are not writing from pain. If you are writing about personal stories in which you have suffered any kind of loss, trauma, pain, or injury (whether that is emotional, financial, physical, mental, or spiritual) be sure to write from a place of healing and not from a place of bitterness. It is ever true that hurting people hurt people. Conversely, the healed can become beacons of hope.

Catherine Brown, *Author Coach-Writing Your Best Nonfiction Book*

vulnerability

Prepare to share that deep and humble scrutiny with your readers. Which requires honesty about the self that few people dare to own up to themselves let alone share.

Readers aren't going to engage with you if you paint only a rosy picture of yourself and those around you. That's not memoir: that's fantasy.

Here's an example. Let's see if you can spot the honest vulnerability in a real-life story from a recent October day.

At the time of this writing, my husband and I are living on our forty-foot sailboat in Mexico's Sea of Cortez. While out in our inflatable dinghy, we heard two men on a nearby sailboat yelling for help.

A woman had been swimming when she slipped under the surface. They had been attempting to perform CPR on the woman but were getting very tired and it wasn't working. They asked us to take her into our dinghy and speed her in to shore and call for an ambulance. They didn't yet have a motor on theirs and they didn't want to waste any more time.

The big man who had been doing the chest compressions lifted what was revealed to be a little wisp of a Mexican woman, unconscious and foaming from the mouth, and passed her to John, my husband. He and I positioned her on the floor of our dinghy. While John drove us as fast as we could safely go, over chop and waves from other craft in the harbour, I knelt over the woman and continued chest compressions. Her eyes were open and glassy.

I used to have a first aid certificate, back in the days when I was a ski patrol, but that was more than thirty years ago and I was horrified to realize how little I remembered about what I was supposed to do. I kept up the rhythmic compressions, worried I was going to break her ribs, but John kept saying, "Harder!" So I kept going.

We ignored the *Slow Down* and *No Wake* signs as we came into the marina area, speeding up to the dinghy dock and screaming that we needed an ambulance NOW. Thank God there were at least six people (many more bystanders!) that instantly helped us haul our dinghy up the launch ramp.

Two young men jumped into the dinghy while I jumped out and they took over the CPR, helping to clear her mouth and doing more compressions.

The ambulance arrived and paramedics took over. They tried to put a tube down her throat to clear her lungs, which helped bring up all kinds of yucky brown stuff that spewed onto the floor of our dinghy.

How am I going to clean that up? I thought. And then my next thought was, *How terrible of me to be worried about that while this woman's life is on the line.*

The main paramedic working on her put his fingers to her neck, looked at his watch, shook his head, and grabbed one of our beach towels and covered her up with it. Leaving her on the floor of our dinghy.

All the official statements and processing and coroners attending and taking photos and removing her body took about three hours. Finally, the coroner approached and thanked us for being available to help, saying that we were now free to take our dinghy.

Which was full of yucky stuff. We threw the beach towels that had covered up her body into the garbage, and some friends brought us some bleach, a bucket, and other cleaning supplies, and we did our best to thoroughly clean and sanitize the dinghy.

Finally we made it back to our boat in the bay. Shaken, sad, drained, but safe and sound.

Did you see it?

The part I'm referring to was around gross stuff spewing from the woman's lungs into our dinghy, and my thoughts around having to clean it up. Would I rather have you think of me as a better person who didn't care as much about the state of cleanliness of my dinghy as much as I cared about the prospect of being able to save this woman's life? Of course.

Would it have made me as relatable had I glossed over that little bit of actual inner dialogue?

No.

We all have those inner voices that say things we aren't necessarily proud of. But they are real. We all have them. Having those inner voices and relaying what they're saying to us is also a far cry from *acting* on what they're telling us.

I did not, for example, scream at the paramedics to remove the woman from my dinghy before they started working on her, lest they get my floor dirty.

To write a memoir that readers will believe, enjoy, interact with, and recommend to others, you need to be brave, confident, and vulnerable enough to show the real you. The good, bad, and sometimes ugly. It's also foundational to character development arcs: you are not the same person after the experience you're writing about in your memoir as you were before it began.

To write the best memoir, you need to be introspective enough to understand the deeper dynamics the events triggered within you, and vulnerable enough to be honest about revealing your less-than-perfect self. That is how readers will relate to you and your story, not when you cover up the living room furniture of your soul in sticky plastic and ask them to take off their shoes.

12

Libel, Slander, and Defamation

*L*ibel and slander are both defamatory: false statements damaging to the person's character and/or reputation.

We'll get more into the definitions and legal bits in a moment. First, full disclosure: I'm not a lawyer, and I haven't been to law school. But my fifteen years as a reporter, writing, publishing, and talking live on television on a daily basis about bad things people do to others, required a basic grounding of the parameters around defamation and involved countless closed-door conversations with in-house counsel. And as a publisher, I'm keen to avoid having any of our Ingenium Books' authors include materials in their books that are potentially actionable. That's the perspective I bring to this matter.

MEMOIR IS OFTEN ABOUT SOME SORT OF TRAUMA INFLICTED upon us by the actions of others. Even if not, we all have conflicts with others that shape who we become. And conflict plays an integral role in every story.

So, I'm expecting you might have a thing or two to say about someone else. And it might not be pretty. You might be tempted to blame, deride, expose, criticize, or condemn. Checking any whining, bitterness, and victimhood at the door, I say go for it. Write about the wrongs and the people playing their part in them. Let 'er rip!

With a big caveat.

And that is to recognize the difference between *writing* and *publishing*. Libel, slander, and defamation only become actionable, meaning there is the *potential* for someone to sue you, *after* you've published what you've written about them.[1]

write without filters

What you write in your first draft is not—I repeat, not—going directly to publishing. There is an entirely new process of vetting, adjusting, and editing where you'll have plenty of time to worry about and rework those areas where you call out your worst enemy and the heinous crimes they have perpetrated against you. And, you'll have the assistance of a professional editor, of course, and perhaps even a publisher that knows what they're doing to guide you in case you fear you're still not on the right side of the libel, slander, and defamation police.

We need to open the heavenly gates between memory and imagination and let your muse run naked through the streets. You cannot find the linguistic and story gemstones without vomiting the slurry first.

There's also a cathartic effect when we write things down, whether it's something we're afraid of, angry or sad about, or even just plain confused. Which means that by writing about these people and the events they're involved in without reservation—in your initial draft—you're helping to process and heal, which are both necessary for the articulation of complete story and character development arcs. You can't leave a reader feeling hopeful and optimistic, or at least like the frayed ends have been cauterized, if you haven't travelled far enough down your own road to rehabilitation.

If you shackle yourself with filters and I'd-better-not-say-this, you're putting yourself behind the eight-ball in a billiards game you can't win. Say what you have to say and edit later.

defining libel, slander, and defamation

As Brette Sember wrote in an article published on the LegalZoom website, "libel and slander are both types of defamation."[2]

Libel is a false statement about someone in writing, including digital writing.

Slander is a false statement about someone made verbally, whether in conversation, in a speech from a podium, or in a televised interview.

Defamation is a false statement framed as fact, in any medium, that results in damage or injury to the character of the person the statement is about.

Notice the word *false* in each definition? In order for someone to have grounds to take legal action against you for something you've written in your memoir, the statement has to be false.

Truth is your best defence.

Remember the discussions we've already had in chapter 10, *Perspectives and Truth*? Here is the one area where I do want you take a closer look at the gap between your truth and the capital T truth. When you're getting ready to publish your memoir and it includes statements presented as fact about another person, you want it to be closer to the capital T truth variety rather than your opinion.

when can someone sue you?

Just because someone can launch a lawsuit doesn't mean they will. They need to hire a lawyer, and lawyers typically prefer to take on cases they have a decent shot of winning, or that the client can pay for in full and up front.

When lawyers do take on a defamation case, they'll have to prove that the false statement(s) in question resulted in harm to a person's good name and character before a court will award damages. Some jurisdictions also require proof that the false statement was made with the intent to cause harm.[3]

Let's say in your memoir you say that Derek is a bank robber. Because of your false statement, Derek loses his job as a cashier at the bank. That's definitely a harm to Derek, losing not just today's paycheques but future income potential as well. If your memoir sells well and readers believe what you've written, a court could award larger damages in the suit Derek could bring against you.

On the other hand, if you know that Derek has changed his name, that he has served jail time after a conviction for bank robbery, and that the bank he works for as a cashier doesn't know about his criminal past, writing about that in your memoir would not be defamatory because a) a court has convicted Derek of bank robbery, and b) the details of Derek's name change are a matter of public record.

emotional truth versus fact

Your emotional truth may differ widely from the capital T truth, and that's okay. Stating your emotional truth is not libellous. Similarly, opinion has a role, as long as you are aware and clear enough to state that what you believe about someone else *is* your opinion and not the capital T truth. Let's look at two different examples.

> The coroner presiding over the inquest wasn't qualified and hadn't read any of the materials in the file. She was an awful person, full of self-importance, and had a complete disregard for me and my grieving family.

In this example, you'd be a little close to the line for my comfort, if I were your publisher. First, it would be a big deal to have an unqualified, unprepared coroner presiding over an inquest. That would say as much about the system as it would about the coroner's lack of credentials and experience.

Here's another way you could write about this, revealing an emotional truth on safer legal ground.

> The coroner walked into the inquest to take her seat at the head of the room. Her hair was held back in a juvenile-looking headband, blond flouncy curls reminiscent of a young Shirley Temple. The growing knot in my stomach hardened with the fear that the outcome of this inquest was in the hands of a woman who didn't look old enough to have graduated from high school. My grief and vulnerability were doing pushups in the background as I squirmed in my chair. I could swear the coroner looked at me with a disdainful smirk.

In the second example, you can see that the author's emotional experience is what's on display, rather than statements masquerading as fact casting aspersions on the character of the coroner. When you reveal your emotional experience, you help your reader empathize and connect with you, worming your way into their heart.

No one can take from you your emotional experience: how you feel is how you feel is how you feel. It's not the capital T truth.

So, write what you want to say. When you're nearly finished, review what you've written and hopefully the benefit of passing time will help you more clearly see where your tone has slipped into the putrid stew of bitterness, whining, or victimhood. Ask yourself if what you've written is the truth. If the answer is yes, proceed with confidence.

MEMOIR WRITER'S CRAFT

Memoir can be every bit as thrilling and engaging to read as superbly-written fiction, maybe even more so, because you know that what you're reading about has really happened. So, as a memoir writer, how do you get your ideas across in a way that will earn your book a place on everyone's list of favourite books?

This section is all about helping you write a memoir that both you and your readers will love.

13

POV: Point of View

*E*verything in your story—every story—is filtered through a point of view.

 The most engaging memoirs are ones in which the author sticks to their POV at the moment of events.

Sarah Chauncey, freelance editor

two meanings of pov

1. POV = OPINION

What you think about a subject and how you present what you think about it, when you're talking with a friend or arguing with a colleague, is a point of view. From this perspective, there can be multiple points of view on any given subject. As a journalist, I needed to keep my writing neutral and without editorial bias, while including as many points of view on the core issue of the story as necessary to help the reader form their own point of view or opinion. Depending on what your memoir is about, this editorial neutrality POV may or may not play a role.

· · ·

2. POV = Narrator's position when describing events

Imagine you are holding a camera and preparing to take a picture. You bring the viewfinder up to your eye. What you see in that viewfinder is your point of view.

When you're pointed in one direction and zoomed in, you would describe only that which is visible within the frame.

If you zoom out, there is more to see and describe, but you see less intimate detail. And attach your wide-angle lens, and you see even more of the big picture, and still less of the intimate detail.

the four types of POV

With narrative POV, we're considering whose story this is (your memoir=your story) along with whether to tell the story in first person (I), second person (you), or third person (he, she, it) POV. And there are two variations of third person POV.

- **First person point of view:** I am *in* the story, describing the things that happened to *me*, when *I* am telling the story. In memoir, first person POV is most common. It's also common in fiction. Because the story details are filtered through a single person's unique POV, they are naturally biased and incomplete. We call this limited: the narrator can't know or share all perspectives on the story. It's their story, not necessarily *the* story. Remember our conversation a couple of chapters ago around perspectives and truth? Example: *I stepped in a puddle on my way to the bank.*
- **Second person point of view.** Written one-to-one, telling the story to *you*. This POV is effective in many types of nonfiction, for example how-to, self-help, or business. It brings a personal, intimate experience to the reader. Second person POV is rare in fiction. Example: *Here's how you avoid stepping in puddles.*
- **Third person point of view, limited.** You'll find the

majority of commercial fiction in third person POV: the story is about **he** or **she**, the narrator is outside the action describing what's going on for a character. Example: *Her feet got wet when she stepped in the puddle on the way to the bank. She noticed the bank manager's look of disdain as she tracked wet sloppiness across the marble floor inside.*

- **Third person point of view, omniscient.** The narrator is still outside the action, and the story is still about **he** or **she**, but the narrator has full access to the thoughts and experiences of *all* characters in the story.

example of third person POV, omniscient

Her feet got wet when she stepped in the puddle on the way to the bank. As she tracked wet sloppiness across the marble floor inside, she noticed the bank manager's look of disdain. She knew this meant her credit application had been denied. Should she just turn around and leave now?

The bank manager had just fired his lazy, sloppy custodian. Who am I going to get to clean up the wet floor right now? I can't leave it like that, *he thought. Then he recognized Mrs. Smith, and he turned back to his desk to pull out the papers she'd need to sign to open up her new line of credit.*

head-hopping: the biggest no-no with POV

I was working with an author on an otherwise promising piece of work, written in third person omniscient. However, she frequently changed up POVs within the same paragraph, even within the same sentence, and was not either able to or unwilling to make the changes to avoid giving her readers whiplash. This is commonly referred to as *head-hopping*. We parted ways.

Let me demonstrate two head-hopping examples for you so you know what to watch for.

*Her feet got wet when she stepped in the puddle on the way to
the bank. As she tracked wet sloppiness across the marble floor
inside, worried about the status of her credit application, the
bank manager looked at her with disdain, wondering who the
hell was going to clean up the mess.*

In the above example, we can see the omniscient narrator in
the first sentence. In the first part of the second sentence, the
narrator is clearly inside the head of the woman with the wet feet,
but in the second half of that sentence the author head-hops by
entering the head of the bank manager.

*The doctor and his patient spent the morning together, each of
them anxious to learn more: the doctor about his patient, the
patient about her condition. George continued trying to pierce
the armour around her memory, wondering who she had been
before the accident. Snippets of scenes from her childhood,
including palm trees, dense jungle, and oppressive heat, were
coming to her, but she couldn't grasp faces, names, or locations.*

In this example, I'm not terribly bothered by the omniscient
narrator's presentation of both doctor and patient in the first
sentence. By the second sentence, the reader is being led to believe
the narrator is drilling down tighter into the doctor's viewpoint.
Still not bothersome. But then the whiplash occurs as the author
switches to what's going on in the patient's head.

If you mix POV too often, you risk losing your reader's trust
and eroding the framework of your narrative. Choose one POV
and stick with it.

POV in memoir

Because it's your memoir, and it's about your (inner) transforma-
tional journey, readers expect your memoir to be written in first-
person point-of-view (mostly).

While your memoir shines light on your inner metamorphosis and the resulting change in how you see the world, as you write about each event, and each scene within the event, aim only to describe the thoughts, feelings, perceptions, and experiences *as they were at the time.*

The danger with the first-person you'll almost certainly employ for your memoir is the temptation to spend too much time in your head, describing only your thoughts and feelings in each situation. Remember: it's not what we *say*, it's what we *do* that counts. There are writers who play with POV, but they are highly skilled and choose to mix up POV for strategic, purposeful reasons.

14

Set the Scene

A scene is any piece of your memoir that involves one or more characters doing or saying something: it's action. Each scene is a mini-story with its own beginning, middle, and end. Any change of location, or time, or the POV character, that signals the start of a new scene.

Setting the scene helps you draw your readers in, making them feel like they're right there with you. Your aim is to pull them out of their world and catapult them into yours—at least, the one you're writing about in your memoir.

purpose

Scene-setting is more effective once you know why the scene is integral to the reader's journey and to your story. A scene's purpose can be to advance the reader's understanding of one or more of the following:

- the character
- the conflict
- the plot (sequence of events)

In life, and in memoir, something happens (action), we respond/react, internally assimilate the event, process what happened, and then we decide what new action we'll take. That flow will look something like this inside each of your scenes:

action > response > assimilation > process > new action

internal and external conflict

Of course there's going to be external conflict: with another person, a place, or a thing.

But some of the most significant forms of conflict happen within ourselves: *I want a meaningful relationship, so why do I keep having these one-night stands?* Or, *I want to be slim, so why do I keep having the grande frappuccino with extra whipping cream?*

Show the reader what's going on inside you at the start of the scene, and show how it has changed by the end of the scene. Following along on the two examples above, perhaps I refuse an invitation into bed, finally starting to respect and honour myself and my long-term desire for a mate. Or, I find that while standing in line at Starbucks I really *do* want the plain, unsweetened green tea because it makes me feel better about how I'm taking care of myself.

When deciding what the inner conflict in your scene is about, consider the following questions: What's your state of mind? What are you struggling with? What don't you understand? Consider the dilemmas, desires, and choices that lay the groundwork for the reader's understanding of where you take them next.

Every scene needs some conflict and tension. If you find yourself writing a scene without either of these, perhaps it doesn't need to be included.

the physical setting

Incorporate elements into your characters' actions that show the reader where your scene is taking place. But don't lump all the physical descriptions of the location into the first paragraph, or even into the same paragraph!

Use action and dialogue to show the reader what she needs to know about where you are.

Let's look at these two options:

Option A.

Our little town had only one dusty main street, and one single-story red-brick bank building. Inside the bank, which smelled of old paper, there were only two teller stalls, and only one office: for the town's only bank manager. He was a smug little prick, knowing as he did the intimate financial details of every resident of the town.

I walked into his office to ask for a loan. He said no.

Option B.

I pulled my car over into one of the many empty angled parking spots right in front of the red-brick bank building. I shut off the ignition and sat there with my hand on my mostly-empty purse, heart thumping, steeling myself for what I had to do.

The smell of old paper hit me as I opened the main doors and walked in. I was the only customer. My inside voice was screaming at me to turn around and get the hell out.

One employee looked up, bored, from behind the vacant teller stalls. "You're here to see Mr. Jones." Her eyes slid to the only office, where I could see the bald-headed Mr. Jones staring at me with contempt. Clutching my purse to my chest, I walked into his office, waiting to be invited to sit.

No invitation came.

"Yes, Mary?" Mr. Jones knew far more about me and everyone else in our small town than I was comfortable with. Some things you just want to keep private, you know? He peered at me over his half-moon glasses.

"I, uh…" He already knew I was about to lose my house. He

already knew I'd lost my job because it had been months since I'd deposited a paycheque. He already knew I was behind on my credit card payments. Was he going to make me beg?

"I was hoping you could help me with a short-term loan, just until I get back on my feet?"

I could feel the beads of sweat forming on my brow. I hoped Mr. Jones didn't notice.

As he leaned back in his squeaky swivel chair, bringing his hands up and interlacing them behind his head, his mouth morphed into a sneer.

Back in the car, a tidal wave of despair sent my head onto the steering wheel, forced sheets of tears down my cheeks, and heaved gasping sobs from my chest. What was I going to do?

The Option B passage above isn't going to win any prizes, but I hope you can see how descriptions of the setting are woven into the action, as opposed to Option A, where it's all lumped into the same paragraph. Which do you think is more engaging for the reader?

the six senses and the weather

Scene-setting descriptions are enriched when you incorporate elements of all five senses: sight, sound, smell, taste, touch. And the sixth sense: intuition. What colour is the light? Is the air moving, and if so, what is the evidence? Do you feel it on your cheek? Is there a smell, either real or triggered by memory? Is there something you're touching, or that obviously has a texture? What is that taste in your mouth? What is your intuition telling you is about to happen?

Weather can bring a cliched ambiance to your narrative— think the Alfred Hitchcock films where it is always a thunderous lightning storm—or it can add to the context in a more subtle way. Perhaps it can be used to contrast what's happening in your scene: a brilliant blue sky and warm summer day and you're getting your heart broken by the love of your life. Too many first time authors I work with forget about the weather entirely, and I think this is a missed opportunity. As you write each of your scenes, ask yourself what the weather was like, what was happening in the sky, what sounds was the weather producing? And if you live in a climate where it snows in winter, can you not smell the snow before it comes?

When you're writing about other characters in your memoir, intersperse (no lumping!) elements of what they look like. Are they wearing perfume or cologne? What's their vocal timbre? When you're around them, do you experience a particular taste in your mouth? Do they touch everything within reach, or remain a safe distance from every surface with their homemade antiseptic spray close at hand?

You can use these scene-setting descriptions to support or to contrast the pivotal emotions and events you're writing about.

Remember that in real life, very little is stagnant. Things are constantly happening, moving, and shifting. Take care that your scene-setting descriptions don't end up feeling like a freeze-frame. Keep them dynamic.

Solid scene-setting skills will also use your *show, don't tell* writing muscles, which is where we're going next.

15

Show, Don't Tell

---

*A*s memoir writers, our aim is to create an *emotional* experience for our readers, rather than a purely *intellectual* one. By *showing* the reader what's happening, how characters are feeling, and the dynamics of their relationships with others, our writing has more depth and impact.

There's a famous quote attributed to Russian novelist Anton Chekov:

 Don't tell me the moon is shining; show me the glint of light on broken glass.

Show, don't tell is one of the often-repeated rules of writing that's among the hardest to master.

why show

When you *show* the reader, you're engaging with her imagination, evoking images in her mind's eye. She'll conjure up, on her own, the colour and texture and emotion and tone that you're trying to impart.

When you *tell* the reader, you make decisions on her behalf, removing them and their imagination from the equation. You're delivering information that, for the most part, requires no interpretation. It's more expedient, but less interesting.

examples of telling

I was angry.

The concrete floor was cold and hard.

She was cute and petite.

Elsa was selfish and inconsiderate.

showing instead

Heat rose up my face, my throat clenched, and before I could stop it the flat of my hand slammed the table so hard his coffee spilled.

I couldn't sit here for long. My bum was going numb and I no longer had feeling in my toes. My eyes scanned the basement for a blanket or pillow, but the small pool of light from the single bulb revealed only more grey.

She could wear anything and look like a million bucks and she didn't have to shop at the Big & Tall Girl stores like I did. Heads turned whenever she walked by. When she smiled, which was often, I wanted to pinch the dimples in her cheeks.

Elsa pouted all through dinner, barely joining in as we sang happy birthday to Tim. She'd thought this was a surprise party for her birthday, even though that was still six months away. As Tim proposed a toast to thank us all for coming, Elsa scraped her chair back like fingernails on a chalkboard and left the table for the bathroom.

tips for showing

Some writers will tell you the only way to show is through dialogue. Dialogue is one way, for sure, and it's effective. But it isn't the only way. We'll start there.

- **Dialogue:** how your character speaks tells the reader plenty about them. Do they use long words and formal greetings, or speak in short, clipped slang, calling the university president "bro"?
- **Setting the scene:** as we discussed in the previous chapter, show your character's perceptions about the physical location by using the six senses. (Remember the weather!)
- **Action:** show readers through action. Instead of "the pelican had a big, grey body, and long beak," how about this: "Turning a graceful glide into a deadly dive, the pelican pierced the sea surface beak first, and came up gulping."
- **Body language:** you may have heard that more than 90 percent of communication is non-verbal, e.g. body

language. The position of the arms, raising of the eyebrows, sweat on the brow, flushing cheeks: all body language that suggest the emotional reaction of a character to another person or event.

signs you're telling

If you're struggling to see where you can overhaul your writing to include more *show* and less *tell*, scan your work for *telling* phrases, called filters, and consider revising:

- I saw
- I heard
- I smelled
- I felt
- I tasted

Note that these are explainer phrases for the five senses. When you use these phrases, you deny the reader the opportunity to apply their own emotional interpretation to what you're writing about, which erects a barrier between your reader and your experience. What we want is to draw them in.

Review your writing and find those sensory-explainer phrases. Instead of using one of these filters, employ visual language and strong verbs. Dig deeper into the specifics and describe *what* you saw/heard/smelled/felt/tasted. If you can do that through action, you get bonus points.

Also watch for tendencies to use labels for emotion:

- happy
- sad
- angry
- elated
- love
- excited

- anxious
- frustrated
- depressed
- etcetera

When you find yourself using one of these labels, try instead to describe the physical signs you or the character exhibit—internally and externally—when they are in the grips of said emotion.

when to tell

If *showing* is more descriptive, more engaging, and results in longer text, *telling* is the opposite. And there are plenty of times *telling* is the right strategy to adopt.

We sometimes need to convey information to the reader that isn't directly furthering the conflict, character arc, tension, or plot. In these cases, telling makes more sense. Do you need to get yourself from point A to point B? Rather than show every detail of your journey from your house to the bank, a single sentence may be the better choice:

I got into the car and headed for the bank.

Yes, it's a mistake to take *show, don't tell* as inviolable. While summary narrative is largely frowned upon, sometimes it's a prudent choice. If *showing* some mundane but necessary information adds no value to the plot/tension/conflict/character arc, *telling* is preferable.

Sometimes, summary narrative can be dispensed with altogether. Readers are smart enough to figure out that if you are at your house in one paragraph, then in the next you're pulling your car into a parking spot in front of the bank, you must have left the house and driven to the bank. A section break can be helpful but even that isn't always necessary.

MEMOIR IS A RICHLY EMOTIONAL JOURNEY: IT WAS emotional for you as you first experienced it, otherwise it wouldn't be worth writing about. And therefore we want to create an equally rich emotional journey for the reader in our retelling. Our *reshowing*, rather.

16

Memoir Dialogue...from Memory

*D*ialogue acts as another hook to draw the reader in. It takes what might otherwise be boring information (expository) and turns it into a mini story. A scene. This entices the reader to continue reading to find out what happened next. Here's what else dialogue will do for your nonfiction work:

- **Dialogue adds realism.** Nearly every event involving people also includes a conversation. Reproducing this conversational exchange helps bring the reader into the room.
- **It helps set the scene.** Dialogue can show us the tangible elements of the place and provide context. It can reveal what led to the event, who was involved, and what's happening now.
- **It tells us more about the characters**. The way people speak can tell us a lot about them. Their accent, for instance, can give away where they come from, their level of education, and so on. The type of slang they use can tell us more about their age and social circles, both past and present. Their speech patterns can tell us about their state of mind.

- **It moves the narrative action forward.** Using dialogue to describe a key event in the narrative can help the reader get a sense of what to expect next. It's a dynamic way of sending the story into a specific direction.

dialogue's emotional impact

Dialogue can help ramp up the emotional impact for your readers. Let's compare these two examples.

Example 1: *Diane was confused when the police arrested her. She didn't know why she was being taken into custody.*

Example 2: *"What are you doing?" Diane was suddenly short of breath. As the policeman pulled her hands behind her back and closed the handcuffs, she couldn't believe this was happening. "Officer, what did I do wrong?"*

In the first example, you'll recognize that we're *telling* the reader what happened. In the second example, dialogue helps us do a better job of *showing* the reader how Diane felt and what she thought.

truth in dialogue

The challenge for memoirists is how to add dialogue while remaining true to the capital T truth. After all, your memoir is the story of what really happened. How can you remember exactly what was said all those years ago? How can you know what was said if you weren't there?

If you're going to invent part or all of the dialogue, doesn't that mean you've just wandered into the realm of fiction? No.

The choice isn't between ensuring there's no daylight between what was actually said and not writing dialogue at all.

So, what should you do? Here are three ways to incorporate dialogue without losing credibility.

actual dialogue

You may find quotes from interviews, transcripts, or court documents. Perhaps you have home movies (dating myself!) or other video with some of your memoir characters speaking.

If you use interviews to conduct research, be sure to take copious and thorough notes or consider recording them and transcribing. This provides a wealth of potential dialogue.

representative dialogue

When you can't quote what the person *actually* said, you create dialogue from what they *may have* said.

Memoirs, biographies, and travelogues often include representative dialogue. Here's when you might want to use representative dialogue:

- When you don't recall the actual words, for instance, but can remember the gist of an important conversation.
- When you weren't there, but you got your information from someone who was.
- Or perhaps you've used real quotes throughout your book, and suddenly, at a pivotal moment in the narrative, there's no recorded dialogue that you can use. A little conjecture here is perfectly fine, as long as the dialogue still represents what could have been said.

To make representative dialogue authentic, consider how the person would really talk. What speech patterns, accent, or phrases do they use? What's the context in which they're speaking? How I talk differs depending on which one of my two cats I'm talking to, to a client, or to my son.

If you're writing representative dialogue involving a person you never met, you might read their letters and journals to get a sense of how they used language. Take note of any phrases or words they were fond of using. Then imagine what they said and how they said it in a given situation.

Most readers will understand that it's impossible for you to know exactly what all the characters in your memoir said. They'll assume that at least some of the dialogue is representative, whether or not they know what it's called.

add a dislaimer

If you're worried about being accused of misrepresentation, you can always add a disclaimer to your book. You can do this in the text itself with phrases like, "I remember Diane saying something along the lines of …"

Or, state in the author's notes section that the dialogue is representative and not verbatim.

what not to do in dialogue

Bad dialogue can damage the quality of your book and your credibility as an author. Let's take a look at the most common mistakes to avoid.

1. **Covering too much.** The main purpose of dialogue is to help move the narrative forward. It should give your readers just enough information to pique their interest. In memoir, your dialogue is going to be based on real conversations. Reproducing the entire conversation is probably too much.

2. **Not covering anything relevant.** Including dialogue simply for the sake of it won't move your story forward. Instead, it can distract from the story you're trying to tell. Before you include dialogue, ask yourself these questions: What is the point of this piece of

dialogue? Does it move the story forward? Does it reveal more about the characters? Does it impart new and relevant information? Is it interesting? If necessary, summarize with expository instead: *We made small talk for a while.* Or, *She showed me around her garden and explained the medicinal properties of each plant.*

3. **Being unrealistic.** It's normal to want to portray some characters in your memoir in either a positive or negative light, depending on who they were to you and their role in the story. But none of us is one-dimensional, we're all flawed, and your dialogue should reveal that. And few people talk in a formal, stilted manner. Also bear in mind that people often make grammatical mistakes when they talk. Don't try to correct their grammar too much, or they'll all start sounding like nineteenth century university professors.

4. **Being too realistic.** Reproducing real dialogue has its own pitfalls. Most people use fillers when they talk: "um," "ah," and so on. Including these can break up the flow of the text and distract from what is being said. The same goes for unstructured trains of thought: people may get sidetracked and go off topic when they talk in real life. This can become very confusing to your readers.

5. **Not setting the scene.** No dialogue happens in isolation. While people are talking, there are many things happening around them. Birds chirp, cars drive past, dogs bark in the distance. The speakers themselves are doing things other than talking, too. They take a sip of their drink, scratch their head, stare into the distance. All of these things help set the scene. *He looked down, dropping his voice to a whisper when he spoke next. "I never thought it would happen to me," he said.*

6. **Spelling everything out.** We can tell a lot about how

someone thinks or feels from what they say. Writers often make the mistake of spelling everything out. For example: *"I'm done here!" he shouted before stomping off. He'd had enough and wasn't going to say anything more on the subject.* The second sentence is superfluous: from the first sentence it's pretty clear that he's not going to say anything more.

7. **Overdoing phonetics.** Different accents can add wonderful colour to a dialogue. However, trying to reproduce them too faithfully can leave you with a string of unintelligible words. Instead, you can add one or two phrases in phonetic spelling to give a sense of the accent and then continue in regular English. For example: *I asked him where the house used to be. He thought for a moment and then pointed towards an open field. "I dinnae. Oor air," he continued in his thick Scottish brogue. "I was just a lad."*

dialogue tags

Dialogue tags are those little phrases like, "she said," "I asked," and "he replied." Their purpose is to tell us who is speaking, not to showcase your extensive vocabulary.

Not including dialogue tags will leave your reader trying to figure out who is saying what, while including them every time someone speaks is distracting and dull. The secret is balance.

Once you achieve this state of balance with dialogue tags, there are still two big potholes to drive your Porsche around, otherwise you'll destroy your suspension.

1. Adverb-y dialogue tags.

An adverb is verb modifier, an "-ly" word we use to communicate emotion and tone. Angrily, sadly, quickly, abruptly, happily.

They *tell* the reader what the character is feeling, when you want to *show*.

"I can't believe you did that," Patrick said angrily.

Angrily is the adverb here and doesn't add value. In fact, it subtracts value because it removes emotion rather than revealing it.

"I can't believe you did that!" Patrick said, his blood boiling.

In this version, the exclamation mark shows you there's emotion behind Patrick's words. And the boiling blood gives you a picture of the physical manifestation of anger. No adverb needed.

2. SAIDISMS

Saidism describes the synonyms that can substitute the word *said. Saidism.* Sounds like *sadism,* and it acts like sadism too: by inflicting pain and humiliation on your writing.

Rather than add interest, resorting to *saidisms* serves only to interrupt the emotional experience of the reader and detract from what's being said.

"Patrick," she exclaimed, "please put that down."

All of a sudden, the focus of this sentence is on the word *exclaimed,* and not on what's being said or why. Instead, you could use punctuation, an additional descriptor to show the speaker's emotional state, or italics.

"Patrick," she said, "*please* put that down."

Stay away from your thesaurus when writing dialogue tags and remember that simple is better. By using "she said" or "he asked," you keep the tag in its rightful place: a supporting actor in the theatre of your memoir, not one who upstages the star.

read, practice, read, practice

The key to mastering dialogue is to practice, read the work of other memoirists, and practice some more. Soon you'll find your own dialogue is popping with life and colour, your narrative arcs are round and healthy, and you and your readers are happy.

17

Active vs. Passive Voice

*W*hy is it better to write in active voice? It's what every writing coach and editor will tell you. But why? And how do you keep from slipping into the nasty habit of passive voice?

First, let's look at what the *active voice* is. It simply means that when you construct a sentence, you do it in this order:

subject > verb / verb phrase > object

For example: *Andy ate all the cookies.*

In this sentence, *Andy* is the subject. The verb or verb phrase is *ate* and the object is *all the cookies.*

In the passive voice, the sentence construction is the other way around:

object > verb / verb phrase > subject

For example: *All the cookies were eaten by Andy.*

See? (Either way, it sucks if you were looking forward to those cookies.)

benefits of writing in active voice

Active voice makes for more concise, less wordy sentences. And less wordy sentences are easier to understand. Active voice sentences are more direct. In the passive voice, it's easier for them to become convoluted. Your tone becomes more conversational and informal.

When you talk, how often do you use the passive voice? Probably not that often at all.

"What happened to the cookies?" Mom asked.
"All the cookies were eaten by Andy."

It's hard to fathom anyone actually speaking this way. Most of us tend to talk in active voice. When you write in active voice, you're writing the way most people speak.

Active voice creates an emotional impact.

The thieves stole Heather's bicycle and all her money.

Don't you immediately feel a sense of anger and shock when reading this? Compare your emotional reaction when the sentence is in the passive voice: *Heather's bicycle and all her money were stolen by the thieves.* The passive voice creates emotional distance.

Active voice creates a sense of immediacy. This can help with pacing.

When you write in active voice you emphasize the actor rather than the action.

Scientific and bureaucratic writing often use the passive voice, since it creates a sense of objectivity and formality. Unfortunately, many nonfiction writers think that they should use the passive voice too. They're writing about facts, after all.

However, even when you're writing about the true events in your memoir, you want to tell a story that people will enjoy reading. If you've ever struggled to stay awake while reading a scientific report written primarily in the passive voice, you'll understand why this isn't the best way to construct your sentences when you want to engage your readers.

how to spot passive voice

How do you know if a sentence is in the passive voice? And how do you write in active voice instead?

1. **Look for phrases containing the word *by*.** This often indicates the passive voice, in which case the words following the word *by* are normally the subject of the sentence. Rewrite your sentence so that the subject comes before the action and the word *by* becomes obsolete. *All the cookies were eaten **by** Andy.*

2. **Look for the past participle.** It doesn't always indicate the passive voice, but passive voice always uses the past participle form of the verb. A past participle is the form of the verb describing a completed action: looked, reached, he was lost, etcetera. For example, *The book was written by a former police officer.* It's easy to identify this sentence as passive voice because of both the past participle and the word *by*. To turn this sentence into active voice, you need to move the subject, *a former police officer*, to the beginning of the sentence so that it's before the verb. Then you need to change the past participle to the appropriate form of the verb. In this case, it will be *wrote* since the sentence is in the past tense: *A former policeman wrote the book.*

3. **Absent subject?** Sometimes the subject isn't present when the sentence is in the passive voice. For example: *In Buddhism, it is believed that life is an endless cycle of death and rebirth.* Who is the subject here? In other words, who believes that life is an endless cycle of death and rebirth? The sentence doesn't explicitly state who believes this. However, we can tell from the

context. We get our clue from the phrase, *In Buddhism*. So, we can safely assume that it's Buddhists who believe that life is an endless cycle of death and rebirth. Therefore, we can rewrite the sentence in active voice this way: *Buddhists believe that life is an endless cycle of death and rebirth.* The context may not always be clear from the sentence itself but from the rest of the text. Then you can use a more general term for the subject. For example, *people, researchers, experts in the field, scientists*, and so on. Sometimes you can even use the general term *they*. Take this common saying, for example: *It is said that life begins at forty.* Since it's such a universal saying, thanks in part to the massive demographic cohort of baby boomers, it's perfectly acceptable to rewrite it like this: *They say that life begins at forty.*

When you read, practice spotting active and passive voice. Write in active voice until you feel really comfortable with it. Then you can break the rules, on purpose and with flair, and write in passive voice only when the circumstances call for it.

18

When to Choose Passive Voice

*T*here is room for passive voice. In fact, I'd argue there are four big reasons you might choose to use passive voice in some instances in your memoir.

First, let's visit some of the reasons passive voice gets a bad rap.

critics of passive voice

Studies[1,2] have found that we tend to use the passive voice when talking about acts of violence. For example: *The student was attacked by three men.* Critics of this way of describing violence say that we're using the passive voice to reduce the crime to something less serious, that we are letting the attackers off the hook.

Check your own emotional reaction when you read the sentence this way: *Three men attacked the student.* The emphasis is now on the three men and what they did: attacking a student. They now seem more culpable, don't they?

Within this criticism and emotional distancing effect lie the very reasons you might consciously choose passive voice, at least in some passages, depending on the subject matter in your memoir.

four reasons to choose passive voice

1. **Emphasizes the action.** Because we don't emphasize
   the person responsible for the action, the action itself
   becomes more important in the reader's mind. In fact,
   often when using the passive voice, we leave out the
   subject altogether. For example: *The water was
   polluted.* At this stage, it's not important to the reader
   who was responsible for polluting the water. What is
   important is the pollution itself.

2. **Creates a sense of anonymity.** When we don't know
   who performed the action, we tend to use the passive
   voice because it allows us to omit the subject. This
   comes in handy when we don't want to reveal, just yet,
   who the guilty party is. It creates anonymity and also a
   sense of mystery. *The water was polluted.* By whom?
   With what?

3. **Fosters objectivity.** Because the passive voice creates a
   sense of emotional distance between the reader and the
   narrative, the reader can become more objective about
   what he or she is reading. This is one of the main
   reasons why scientific reports are often written in the
   passive voice. While the journalism writing coaches
   encourage active writing, especially in broadcast, there
   are often legal reasons that underpin the choice of
   passive voice. For example: *The water was polluted by a
   nearby mining operation.* In Canada, where I was a
   journalist, the passive form of this statement is legally
   safer. A court hasn't yet proven, or the mining
   company hasn't yet claimed responsibility, that a
   specific mining company is culpable for the pollution
   in this body of water. *The ABC mining operation
   polluted the nearby water.* After all, when you read the

sentence in the active voice, you feel almost ready to go picket at the mining operation's offices, don't you?

4. **Imbues authority.** If the active voice sounds more conversational, the passive voice sounds more formal. Readers tend to perceive this formality as more professional and more authoritative. It sounds like the author knows what he or she is talking about.

how do you decide?

When you're considering whether or not, or when, to use the passive voice when you write nonfiction, ask yourself these questions:

- What is the message I want to convey?
- What do I want my readers to feel?
- Is there a reason I might want to create emotional distance?
- Do I want my readers to feel anything at all?
- Do I want to emphasize the action over the person/thing doing the action?
- Is there a benefit to my creating a sense of anonymity and mystery over who is taking the action?
- Do I want my writing to be more conversational, or more authoritative?

So, you're now armed with the knowledge that there are, in fact, good reasons to choose to use passive voice when you write memoir. It's tied to your objective for your book, who your reader is, what experience you want to create for them, and the impression you want to leave with them when they're done. Just beware that you can mix up passive and active voice, based on the topic and action and the emotional involvement you want your reader to have at the time.

19

What's Your English?

*Y*ou want your writing to reflect your authentic voice, as long as the tone is appropriate to your topic (you don't want, for example, to use a light-hearted, cheeky tone for a book on a serious topic, such as child abuse, or a serious, big-worded and formal tone for a book with a humorous or satirical point to make). However, it pays to be aware of the nuances of your English.

Where you were born, raised, educated, and live will dictate which of the Englishes you speak and write. When you're writing memoir, it's a balancing act between remaining authentic with your own English and being sure your readers will understand you.

 When you get to the robot, you turn left. You'll see the restaurant on your right. Watch out for the taxis! I'll come just now, then we'll have a cooldrink. As a South African living in a community of expats from all over, I quickly learned that people didn't always understand what I was talking about. South African English looks like English, sounds like English, is English … but sometimes it seems like it's from another planet. Incidentally, a *robot* is a traffic light;

taxis normally refer to minibuses used as a form of public transport and their drivers are notoriously reckless; *just now* indicates some vague point in the future; and a *cooldrink* is a soft drink, a soda or pop.

Linell van Hoepen, Ingenium Books contributor

the wonder and challenge of English

Wherever English is spoken, it develops its own unique form. It's not only about *harbour* versus *harbor*, but about the words and phrases you'll only find in your own area. I love hearing someone speak their own English, and in many cases I learn so much about them just from a few words. I can tell if a Canadian is from the West Coast, one of the prairie provinces, Eastern or Atlantic Canada. Pronunciations will reveal broad geographic influences: no mistaking someone from the UK, Australia, the deep South of the US, or South Africa.

But it's about more than pronunciation. A *cabin* in British Columbia is a *cottage* in Ontario. A *cupboard* in Montreal and Ontario is a *closet* in the West. *Minced meat* is ground beef in Montreal and a sweet and savory Christmas pie or tart filling in the West. My husband, from Montreal and therefore influenced by the French, will say, "I'll pass by," whereas in most of the rest of Canada we'd say, "I'll come by," or "I'll drop by." A *boot* in the UK is the *trunk* of a car in Canada and the US. A *soda* in parts of the US[1] is a *pop* in Canada. A *thong* in many countries is a style of women's underwear but in Australia, the US, and parts of Canada it's a care-free summer sandal often called a *flip-flop*. Both fit the technical definition *thong*, as does a narrow strip of leather, but the common usage differs depending on where you are. And on it goes.

This is also the difficulty of English. When you're writing your memoir, you'll want to be conscious enough of those influences in your English so that, where there might be confusion in a reader who does not live across the street, you can choose language more universally understood.

authentic dialogue in the character's English

In your memoir, which you'll recall is a form of narrative nonfiction, you might want to write dialogue that lets your characters, including you, speak their natural form of English. If needed, you can explain potentially unfamiliar terms after the dialogue. For example:

> *"I dropped my soda on the kitchen floor." My friend was on her hands and knees, swabbing a wide swath of the linoleum. It took me a nanosecond to realize she meant her pop, full of sugary stickiness, and it was going to take her more than a few minutes to clean it up.*

choosing to go neutral

Where it doesn't make sense to use dialogue, consider choosing a more neutral form of English. Avoid slang and regional expressions. Instead, opt for more generally-known terms.

Instead of using the Australian *barbie* or the South African *braai*, use the more well-known *barbecue*, for example. Instead of saying I'll "knock you up," which while innocuous in the UK means to impregnate in Canada and the US, opt for the more generic "wake you up."

Luckily, in our increasingly interconnected world, some regional terms are universally understood. Most people know that what the British call aubergines, for instance, are what is known elsewhere as eggplants. Except in India and South Africa, where they're called brinjals!

be aware of differing sensitivities

Not everyone attaches the same meaning to a certain word. If you're not mindful of this, you may inadvertently cause offence.

> If I'm writing about South Africa's ethnic groups, for instance, I'll always explain right from the start that the term "Coloured" refers to someone who is either of mixed racial ancestry, a descendant of the Khoisan people, or a descendant of slaves brought from the East Indies some three centuries ago. I do this because I know that in the United States, the word is considered offensive when describing a person.
>
> Linell van Hoepen, Ingenium Books contributor

It's your memoir, which means you get to decide what the right balance is between authenticity and clarity, unless you're working with a traditional publisher who dictates your approach to English usage. Making a conscious decision from a place of understanding the ramifications of your choice is an empowered place to be.

20

Plain Language

---

*W*hile you may be tempted to show off your great vocabulary, you need to remember that, first and foremost, you're trying to communicate *effectively*. If nobody understands the words you use, how will they understand your message?

Simplifying your language will get the message across more effectively. It will also make the text more conversational, as if you're talking directly to your reader. And it will keep your book from becoming dull.

Using plain language doesn't mean you're dumbing down your message. You can still explain complicated concepts. Now, however, you're doing it in a way that your readers are more likely to understand.

tips for writing in plain language

- **Use active voice.** As we've discussed, it's more conversational than passive voice and easier to understand. Passive voice, in contrast, can make your book sound like it was written by a little grey man, in a grey suit, in a grey government office.

- **Use simpler words.** How often do you use words and phrases like *consequently* instead of *so*, *such as* instead of *like*, or *discombobulate* instead of *baffle* in everyday conversation? (Full disclosure: I love the word *discombobulate*.)

- **Avoid jargon.** Just because you understand the meaning of a term doesn't mean that your readers will. If there's a simpler or more common synonym for the term, use it. If you can't avoid jargon, explain what the term means. Remember that slang is a form of jargon. If there is a different, more generally-known synonym for the term, use it. For example, doctors understand *hypertension* but people who don't work in the medical field may be more likely to understand *high blood pressure*.

- **Write out abbreviations and acronyms**, at least the first time you use them. For example: The International Labour Organization, or ILO, is an agency of the United Nations that focuses on improving labour conditions around the world.

- **Use shorter sentences.** Stick to the main idea in each sentence. To avoid monotony, vary the length of your sentences. However, try to keep them to no longer than twenty words.

- **Avoid nominalizations.** Nominalizations are those nouns we form from a verb: *usage* from *use*, *formation* from *form*, as examples. Nominalizations make your writing sound overly formal. They can also be difficult to understand.

- **Remember your audience.** In planning your book, you've already thought about who you want to read it. Maybe your target audience is made up of stay-at-home parents, or students, or young people working their way up the corporate ladder. Whoever it is, take into account things like their likely level of education, whether English is their mother tongue, and their prior knowledge of the subject you're writing about.

- **Write to one person.** As authors, we tend to think of our reading audience in terms of the *many*. *"Now that all of you are sitting down reading this book..."* Think about what your reader is doing while reading. It's just them, alone, and your book. One person. One to one. Write as if you're talking to them. Use *I* or *we* when referring to yourself, for instance. Use *you* when addressing your readers.

You probably know the feeling: you read something, probably more than once. And you find yourself asking, "Could you explain it again, but in English this time?" You don't want this to happen to your readers.

The solution is to *write in plain English.*

21

Perfectionism Run Amok

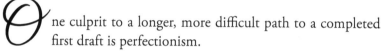

*O*ne culprit to a longer, more difficult path to a completed first draft is perfectionism.

The first draft of your memoir is supposed to be imperfect. In fact it's supposed to be downright horrible. I've heard them called *puke drafts*. Stinky, messy, unorganized, riddled with error, first drafts are diamonds in the rough.

A first draft is not a finished book, and it's not supposed to be. It's just the first draft. And no one but you has to read your first draft.

The publish-ready version of your memoir won't start to appear until you and likely one or two or even three other editorial professionals have worked it through. And that's not because you're a beginner. Every writer starts with a cruddy first draft.

 Every writer you know writes really terrible first drafts, but they keep their butt in the chair. That's the secret of life. That's probably the main difference between you and them. They just do it. They do it by prearrangement with themselves. They do it as a debt of honour.

Anne Lamott, American poet and novelist

first drafts and unrealistic expectations

Good writing takes practice. And it takes time. Good writing is almost never produced in the first draft. The first draft of your book is just bones. It provides the frame, the connections, and an evolving shape that only later starts to resemble the finished book.

Think of your first draft as the next step forward from the outline. Now, not all authors start by writing an outline, and that's fine. We do take the authors we coach through a process that at least begins with an outline, as we find it much easier for an author to *see* their book take shape even before they do much writing.

The concept here is to give yourself permission to let the first draft behave like a more detailed version of an outline. There will be missing pieces. There will be errors, and typos, and gaps in your research. It will be awful, and that's how it is supposed to be. Embrace all this imperfection!

getting it all down

It's hard to get it all down. It's hard not to keep editing the previous paragraph, and the previous chapter, and it's hard not to re-read what you wrote yesterday before you start your writing for today. I admit that I succumb to these temptations more often than is good for my productivity. Ugh.

You must make yourself move forward with your first draft, in whatever way makes sense for you. That might mean writing your story chronologically, start to finish, in the order in which significant events occurred. Or it might mean you take the biggest parts of the story and write those first, then fill in the blanks with the other stuff that you need for the story to make sense. It might mean starting with an outline, and you write what strikes your fancy from that outline every time your butt hits the chair.

If any of the advice in the preceding chapters on POV, scene-setting, show don't tell, dialogue, or active versus passive voice, for example, seem to be slowing your writing down, give yourself permission to *just write*. Get the story down. You will come back after the first draft has had a nice rest in a dark drawer and you and your fresh eyes can take a new look at what you've written, beginning to shape it into the memoir of its destiny.

WRITING PROCESS

*E*very writer approaches their work differently: there is no right or wrong environment, method, or speed. In this section we explore what writing process might work for you.

22

Your Writing Approach

*J*ust as we all have our own unique personality traits as human beings, as writers we have our own personalities too. These personalities dictate the approach we take to the act of writing.

Knowing the range of approaches in advance will help you handle the roadblocks that will arise (they always do, for every writer) as you're on your writing journey.

the fast writer

If you glance down at the keyboard when you're writing and see only a blur where your fingers are supposed to be, you're probably The Fast Writer. You'll experience spurts where you know exactly what you want to say and you simply let it fly.

I tend to fall in the category of The Fast Writer. In part I write fast because I type fast. I cut my teeth on writing quickly as a television reporter with multiple deadlines every single day. Researching and gathering interviews and other materials for each story took the lion's share of the time I had available between receiving my assignment and my on-air slot, so I had to write fast. Were my stories perfect? Oh goodness, no. But, as my very first news director said after I'd missed my slot on the 5:00 p.m. news one day while I perfected something in the editing suite, "It's no good to anybody if it isn't on the air."

If you find that you finish tasks fast, experience intense bursts of high productivity, and are never at a loss for words, you're probably a fast writer.

potential roadblocks for the fast writer

In my experience, one potential roadblock is that when the ideas aren't coming in fast, I have a very hard time forcing myself to sit at the computer and write. It means I sometimes go days without getting any significant writing done on a project.

Another roadblock might be losing track of the structure or story arc. In this way, you might need to embrace elements of The Pantser, below, and give yourself permission to write where inspiration takes you and clean it up later.

And The Fast Writer will need an excellent editor at the other end—but that is true of every writing approach and every writer.

the plotter

Ah, The Plotter. If you feel more comfortable starting your writing process by developing a detailed outline, timeline, and doing detailed character sketches, you're a plotter.

For The Plotter, the writing only begins once this preparatory framework is complete. And the writing: oh my goodness! No one, and I mean NO ONE, will see The Plotter's draft manuscript until they've gone through it several times themselves.

Plotters tend to dislike spontaneity or surprises, and they love to have all social plans scheduled on their calendars weeks in advance. Heaven help the friend who needs to reschedule last minute.

potential roadblocks for the plotter

The Plotter may find themselves stuck on how to handle a new idea or scene that arises after the outline is crafted and there isn't an obvious place for it. Try creating an extra folder for new ideas, or space at the end of the outline, so you can keep the writing going without always needing to figure out where something is going to fit perfectly.

Another roadblock that may be more likely for The Plotter is the propensity to keep going back over the first drafts of the first few chapters, self-editing to death the early parts of the memoir before they've written the first draft of the entire manuscript. I always advise against any self-editing at all before there is a complete first draft precisely because it can become a swirling vortex with a gravitational pull from which there is no escape. And there is no way to finish a book if you can't finish the first draft of a manuscript.

the pantser

How I would love to be The Pantser. At least when it comes to my writing. I'm good with go-with-the-flow spontaneity on my personal calendar but I cannot begin writing without first putting together a solid outline.

All The Pantser needs to have in order to start writing is an idea. Maybe even just the seed of an idea, not yet germinated. Then, they're off. The Pantser doesn't need an outline before they can begin writing, and they don't stress when they don't know what's coming next.

In case you haven't figured this out one yet, The Pantser is so-named because they epitomize the expression *fly by the seat of your pants*.

You might be The Pantser too if any of the following resonate:

- I don't like making travel or vacation plans too far in advance
- I'm comfortable with one-way travel tickets so I can sort out the timing and method of my return later, and
- I don't feel rested unless I get one full day a week where I don't have to make any plans.

potential roadblocks for the pantser

It's possible for The Pantser to have too many ideas and the initial draft doesn't hang together well. The free-flowing act of writing may result in The Pantser losing sight of their original focus, story-line, or even their purpose for writing the memoir. It can be difficult to write for the right reader, and as such may lead to a larger, more extensive editing process that adds time to the project.

the idea generator

A notepad and pen or sticky notes are constant companions of The Idea Generator because ideas about stories, characters, situations, or examples are coming to them all the time, at every moment of any given day. If they don't make a note of them, they may forever lose track.

potential roadblocks for the idea generator

Idea Generators don't often suffer from writer's block, but their desks (or desktops) will be littered with manuscripts in various stages of completion. They're easily distracted by the next great idea and often need an intervention to finish their manuscript and to help them take it through to publishing.

the word nerd

The Word Nerd sleeps with a thesaurus under their pillow. They love a delicious turn of phrase and can get lost for hours tinkling and tweaking and fine-tuning the perfect prose.

potential roadblocks for the word nerd

Word Nerds may suffer more frequently from writer's bock, or if not a block, then a very slow word count per hour. It can venture into the territory of obsession if the Word Nerd isn't careful. An antidote, if you suspect your writing productivity is grinding to a near-halt as you search for the perfect word, is to step back and ask how you'd describe this to a friend or neighbour? And tell yourself you can come back to find the perfect word later.

WHICH WRITER APPROACH DO YOU MOST IDENTIFY WITH? What do you think will be likely to get in your way as you work to write your memoir? How might you plan in advance to handle the challenges that will arise—challenges always arise during the writing process—so that it is a small bump in the road and not a major derailment?

23

Writing Pace and Motivation

*F*or some, the process of writing is easier than for others. However, there is always a challenge involved with writing regardless of your level of skill and experience. One of those challenges is how to stay motivated through what is always a harder, longer endeavour than we think when we set out. The fact is: it takes dedication, focus, and mental and emotional energy to keep making writing progress on your memoir on a daily basis.

Blank page syndrome, more often called writer's block, is going to happen to you—if it hasn't already. Let's look at a few ways you can boost your motivation and get your creative juices flowing with less laborious effort.

keep your eye on the prize

Why are you writing in the first place? What is the reason you write? What do you want to achieve with your writing?

You want to be clear about these motivating factors and keep them front and centre.

Jot the answers to these questions on little sticky notes and put them in prominent places where you'll see them: on the fridge, the bathroom mirror, in the middle of the steering wheel of your car.

The more you can remind yourself of the reason, or reasons, you want to write your memoir in the first place, the easier it will be to stay motivated when writing.

schedule time for writing only

You probably use your calendar to book the appointments you have with other people. Use it for yourself! As a writer, you often have many other things going on that need your attention in addition to the actual writing itself. This may include administrative tasks, marketing tasks, organizational tasks, and more.

Schedule your writing-only time and protect it as the most important thing on your calendar. Don't even think of calling, emailing, or reading other unrelated material. You need to remain focused during the writing-only portion of your work. If you can do this, eventually you'll be pleased with the progress you make over time, which means it will be easier to stay motivated when writing. You'll *want* to push forward.

Sometimes family, friends, and even coworkers may not realize there are time slots in the day, your writing-only time, where you must remain undistracted and undisturbed to get your work done. Let them know about these times, so they can positively participate in your quest to stay motivated when writing by staying out of your way.

write early in the morning or late at night

If you're not a morning person then don't try to schedule your writing at five o'clock in the morning like I do. Not sure? Test it out by setting aside a certain segment of time in the morning, like right before or right after breakfast, to begin clack-clacking those keys.

If you're a night owl, schedule your writing-only time late. You'll encounter little to no distractions, no phone calls and fewer family obligations at night. If this is you, my hat is off. My brain ceases to function coherently at about six o'clock in the evening so it does me no good whatsoever to schedule my writing-only time late in the day.

establish small daily goals

Breaking up your work into smaller segments can help you make progress with much less effort. You might set a goal to write a thousand words each day. That might get broken down further into a number of words per hour. This works better for me than setting a weekly word-count goal, which gives me the opportunity to skip a day, or two, or three, because I have a whole week to hit my target.

create a distraction-free writing zone

My husband John uses headphones and plays his favourite lyric-free music to cut out extraneous noise, making it more difficult for me to interrupt by opening up a conversation with him (but not impossible, haha). But I don't need the same thing to write: fifteen years of writing to deadline in very noisy newsrooms means I can get down to it in all kinds of settings. The trick for you is to know what kind of environment you need, what kinds of distractions interrupt your writing flow, and if necessary, experiment.

Many writers find their motivation and productivity is supported when they find a safe writing space, whether it's a particular room, coffee shop, outdoor setting, or some other setting.

Turn off your phone, or at least turn off the notifications. This will help you respect your writing-only time while allowing you to respond to matters that really do need your urgent attention.

reward yourself

Deliberately setting rewards for yourself during the course of your writing project may help you stay motivated when writing on a schedule. For instance, treat yourself to a walk, yoga session, or a hot bubble bath after you've completed a writing goal.

If you have a nice reward waiting for you on the other side of a pre-determined block of writing time you might find it easier to reach the finish line and your writing goals.

use a journal

Carry a journal, notepad, or even an audio recorder so you can capture your thoughts as they strike you, whether you're on the go or at the office. I've never known a great idea for my writing to appear only when I'm ready to write it down. You never know when a flash of inspiration may hit. The fact you've captured these ideas can give you a boost of added motivation and make you eager to sit down for your next block of writing-only time.

don't edit until you've finished the first draft

There are varying opinions on this, but if you're finding yourself not making progress toward your completed first draft as quickly as you'd wanted or hoped, it may be because you're starting today's writing session by editing yesterday's work. This is bound to muck you up in a pit of quicksand. Going back and forth between writing and editing can cause you to lose focus, break your creative flow, and hinder your motivation.

DON'T BE AFRAID TO TRY DIFFERENT APPROACHES TO SEE what helps keep you motivated and making progress.

24

Your Author Coach

*T*he three elements of ANY achievement, whether launching a business or getting your degree or writing your book, are:

1. Knowledge
2. Experience
3. Mentoring or coaching.

Whether you've mastered these *best memoir* basics or you're still honing your craft, there's no question that the most effective way to catapult your writing—in terms of quality, productivity, and completion—is to hire an author coach.

A good coach will provide you with specific feedback, act as an accountability partner, keep an eye on your project timelines, and take some of the solitude out of what is an otherwise solitary endeavour. Be sure to hire a coach that is familiar with your genre and that you feel a good connection with. You'll want to be comfortable being vulnerable (it's writing, after all) and to accept feedback designed to make you a better writer.

There are nutrition coaches. Leadership coaches. Career coaches. Life coaches. Have you noticed how the people who tend to work with coaches always seem so... together? And you wonder why they, of all people, think they need a *coach?* They appear at the top of their game precisely because they have a coach. Imagine a talented tennis player who wants to win Wimbledon. The player will have a tennis coach who will practise with them, work on technique, and correct little problems before they become big habits. Their coach will set a practice schedule, provide nutrition advice, and help to keep the player mentally focussed. The tennis coach may become a confidante, shoulder to cry on, and cheer-leader all wrapped into one.

Working with an author coach is no different.

what is an author coach?

While every author coach will have a slightly different set of strengths, preferences, and process, a professional author coach will guide you through the writing process, from the first seeds of an idea to the finished manuscript, and perhaps beyond.

Helping you achieve your writing goals is the goal of the author coach. Depending on where you are on your author journey, their assistance may include:

- Helping define your ideal reader
- Working up an outline and providing advice on the structure of your book
- Identifying story or logic gaps you'll want to fill
- Giving feedback on your writing style
- Creating a project plan for your book
- Helping you make decisions about things like distribution options or editors, proofreaders, or designers.

when you need an author coach

I may be biased, but based on the concept of every industry or sector's top performers, every author will benefit from a coach, regardless of their skill or proficiency level.

If you're just starting to work on your first book, you need an author coach. If you've already published one or more books, you need an author coach. If you strive to improve, achieve more, drive more sales, you need an author coach.

The right author coach at the right time is always a good idea. It's never too late.

what to look for in an author coach

What you look for in an author coach depends first on your own assessment of what you want and what you need.

- Know where you're at with your writing skills and where you think you want to improve.
- Know what your book needs.
- Know your personal preferences. Are you more comfortable working with a man? A woman? Will internet calls via Skype or Zoom work for you, or will you need to meet in person?
- What's your budget? No sense aiming for Wimbledon when your budget demands you spend more time at the public courts down the street.

finding your author coach

Finding potential author coaches to interview starts with a simple Google search. It's easy. The Alliance of Independent Authors' (ALLi) Facebook group and their approved partner lists are also great places to look. There are actually lots of choices for you out there. Here are a few things to watch for.

- **Experience:** look for someone with a proven track record. You'll want to be able to check references, so ask for contact information and permission to reach out to past clients.
- **Genre:** find author coaches who have worked with your genre before. For example, we only offer nonfiction author coaching services. We read lots of fiction (as well as nonfiction of course) but our professional specialty is nonfiction. Look for specialization that matches you and your book.
- **Personality and energy alignment:** ask questions, engage in conversation, and see if the author coach feels like a fit. Your work together could last several months to a year. And, your author coach will likely deliver feedback that might feel like a fiery eighty-mile-per-hour serve that blows past your waiting racket like an F16 fighter jet. You want to be sure your author coach can give you objective advice and criticism without crushing your soul. Don't make it harder on yourself than it has to be and choose someone you're immediately comfortable with.

what should you expect?

Once you've chosen your author coach, you will work together to come up with a strategy tailor-made for your book project. The work plan might look something like this.

MEETING #1:

- Content strategy and book focus.
- Your ideas for the book, why you want to write it, what you hope to accomplish.

- You may begin to carve out the broad strokes of a book outline.
- You might receive your first writing assignment (related to the book).

MEETING #2:

- Discussion leading to reader identification (a key element most indie authors miss!).
- A deeper dig into the content to include in your book.
- Feedback and assessment of your writing assignment from meeting #1.
- Your second writing assignment.

MEETING #3:

- How to set a purpose for each section and chapter.
- Feedback on writing assignment #2.
- And more. You get the idea.

Your first few sessions with your author coach might look a little different.

Whatever the frequency, you'll have regular sessions with your author coach – once every two weeks, for instance – while you're writing your book. During these sessions, you'll discuss what you're doing right and what needs to change.

Be wary of author coaches who agree with everything you have written. You're not going to improve if all you get is, "That's fantastic!"

What your coach won't do is write your book for you. That's your job.

25

Re: Vision, Revision

*a*t last comes the question of what to do with your first draft. I cannot tell you this part will be easy: that would be a flat-out, bald-faced, snake-in-the-grass lie.

It's true you have nothing if you can't get your first draft written. It's also true that your first draft is still nothing. It needs you to don the cape of your other writer-half: the self-editor.

the self-editor

Your editor self is not to replace a professional editor, which you will most certainly want to engage once you have exhausted the limits of your self-editing prowess. But that's not what we need to talk about now. Remember when I told you, back on page one, that writing our truth requires bucketloads of courage, and that writing memoir is not for the faint of heart?

Well.

If *writing* memoir requires us to be brave in the face of our fallibility, flaws, defects, and culpability as they relate to the events of our past, we now need to summon up the courage to face the flaws and defects strewn across the pages of our first draft, like trash littering the ground after an outdoor rock concert. *This* field of trash we do *not* wish to put on display for the world to see.

After you've put your first draft away in a dark corner for a time, whether a day or week or two, rolling around in the pride and accomplishment of completing your first draft, you'll dust off your britches, take your first peek at your work, and be hit in the solar plexus by the horrid blandness of your manuscript. Just like every other writer and author there ever was or ever will be.

You're in good company.

The very act of editing our own writing requires us to have the courage to stare down the *facts* of our craft, to painstakingly rework and tune and tweak and cut and expand, so that our writing, our memoir, our story comes through better, clearer, more tantalizing. Ready for the reader we so carefully defined back in chapter four.

self-editing roadmap

If you're unsure where or how to start your first pass of self-editing, here's what I suggest.

1. Print a hard copy, take it to your favourite print shop and have it spiral bound with heavy plastic front and back covers.

2. Sit with a pencil or pen, pink if you have it (wait, that's *my* current colour obsession), and read. Read, read, read. Make notes in the margins, circle phrases or paragraphs. But no actual editing in the electronic document until you've read the whole thing top to bottom.

3. Check the truth you've spilled onto the pages: is it true to your perception of your truth? Have you filtered, massaged, or adjusted the truth out of fear (whether conscious or subconscious) that someone will remember things another way?

4. Have you adequately portrayed the emotional and psychological conflicts raging within you? Are you bravely showing the real you, including the good, bad, and sometimes ugly? Does your story show how the events in your memoir have changed you, how you've grown?

5. Does the structure hold together? Does it do the story justice? Will your reader be able to follow? Does the structure support the creation of the emotional involvement you intended for the reader?

6. If you have decided you need to make structural changes, you may do that before you begin the rest of the self-editing process. Resist getting tangled in the tall swamp grass of micro-editing at this point, just stick to making the structure work.

7. Begin to work now paragraph by paragraph, page by page, chapter by chapter. Use your own margin notes from your hard copy. Review each of the section three chapters in this book, and improve your POV, scene-setting, showing, dialogue, active voice, and plain language.

8. Put the new first revision draft away in its dark corner for a rest. After the allotted time, when both you and your manuscript, which by now will have taken on a life of its own, are ready for another thorough review. Repeat these steps.

still not done

You'll recall that earlier I mentioned that it's normal practice for authors to ask family and friends to review an early draft. You may be ready for this now. I'd suggest being clear with them about what you want them to look for, and what you are not asking for. It can be helpful to tell them you want to know if the story is engaging, what emotions they felt, and whether anything jumped out at them as either unclear, missing, or too detailed. You may wish to tell them you are not looking to them for a fact check, that this is your memoir with your perceptions of things as they happened to you.

Regardless of whether you choose to share an early read with family and friends, you will certainly be ready to engage with a professional editor. And, be prepared for that editor to take you through a new version of the process I've outlined in the above steps.

I did mention that writing memoir is not for the faint of heart, remember?

knowledge is power

While the path to writing the best memoir you can is often buried in mucky foliage, my intention is that *The Best Memoir* becomes your personal pair of rubber hip-waders.

If you've embraced what I've called the toughest, most important part, which is the guts to sit in a chair next to your most vulnerable, self-reflective self, then I do believe you are ready.

Happy writing!

If You Enjoyed The Best Memoir

*I*f you enjoyed *The Best Memoir*, please consider leaving a brief review on Amazon, by clicking this link or typing it into your browser: mybook.to/thebestmemoir.

You could also leave one on the publisher's website, Goodreads, or with the retailer where you bought the book.

Reviews are important to authors. They're even more important to other readers, like you, who rely on what readers before them have thought about a book as they look for that perfect resource.

Your feedback doesn't have to be long or detailed. Just a sentence saying what you enjoyed or how the book helped.

Please accept my thanks if this is something you'd like to do.

BONI WAGNER-STAFFORD

Acknowledgements

I'm grateful for the love of words that has prompted the universe to deliver a life and experience that includes the amazing privilege of co-founding Ingenium Books. It's an enriching honour to work with our authors on their books. I don't know what gives me more pleasure: working on these inspiring, heartbreaking, and heartwarming stories, or building the lasting relationships with the authors. Either way, I'm humbled at my good fortune.

I could not have written this book with any confidence had I not taken two dozen authors through the development, writing, editing, and publishing journey with their books, and in particular these memoirists: Yvonne Caputo, Dina Marie Schweisthal, C.A. Gibbs, Cynthia Barlow, and Denise Collins. My experience and perspective has been invaluably enhanced through my work with authors on other sub-genres of nonfiction too, both published and as yet unpublished: David Reeve, David Rhodd, Lauren Clucas, Gwyn Teatro, Lisa King, Alison Rapping, Orna Ross, Henrik Mondrup, Pranathi Kondapaneni, Heidi Hackler, Tricia Jacobson, Morenike McFaal, and others.

Thanks to my team of beta readers for *The Best Memoir*: Anne

Janzer, Yvonne Caputo, Charlotte Burnham, Cynthia Barlow, David Morris, and Dan Holstein.

Thanks to Linell van Hoepen, Trina Holt, and other Ingenium Books' team members for their valuable contributions to the sparks for some of the ideas I've included here. I must also thank Jessica Bell for her inspiring cover design work with us at Ingenium Books, Amie McCracken for proofreading, and to our go-to stable of professional editors including Rachel Small and Denise Willson. I learn something new from these dedicated pros every day.

Thanks to those kind-hearted and like-minded folks who have given me their permission to quote from their work: Catherine Brown, Tasha Eurich, John Newell, Sarah Chauncey, and Anne Lemott.

And finally, thanks to my husband and business partner, John, for being so incredibly awesome and supportive in all things, in and outside the business, on and off the boat, and sharing in the journey called life.

About the Author

Photo by Miguel Soto

Boni Wagner-Stafford is co-founder of Ingenium Books, a hybrid publisher of outstanding nonfiction.

As a publisher, Boni also offers one-on-one author coaching to nonfiction authors, in particular memoir, and also in the sub-genres of business, self-help, personal development, and journalistic nonfiction.

As an award-winning former Canadian journalist, Boni covered politics, government, social and economic policy, organized crime, and more. She later held senior management roles in government where she led teams responsible for media relations, issues management, and strategic communications planning.

As an entrepreneur, Boni has muddied her hands in the trenches with one-page strategic plans, cash-flow forecasts, developing purpose and core values, franchise structures, sales targets, and marketing and differentiation.

Boni has been at the controls of a helicopter, canoed in the wild backcountry of Northern Ontario, jumped out of an airplane, sang on stage with Andrea Bocelli and Christopher Plummer (not at the same time), and grew up skiing in the Rocky Mountains. She has lived in more than seventeen different cities/towns in Canada, Mexico, and France and spends as much time as possible on her sailboat, which is also named *Ingenium*.

Learn more about us at ingeniumbooks.com.

Additional Reading

Aspiring memoirists and writers may find inspiration in the following additional reading.

Black, Sacha. *Anatomy of Prose: 12 Steps to Sensational Sentences (Better Writer Series)* (Atlas Black Publishing, 2020)

Brown, Catherine. *Author Coach: Write Your Best Nonfiction Book* (Independently published, 2020)

Janzer, Anne. *Get the Word Out: Write a Book That Makes a Difference (*Cuesta Park Consulting, 2020)

Jenkins, Jerry. *Writing for the Soul: Instruction and Advice from an Extraordinary Writing Life* (Writer's Digest Books, 2006)

Lamott, Anne. *Bird by Bird: Some Instructions on Writing and Life (*Anchor, 1st edition, 1995)

Penn, Joanna. *How to Write Nonfiction (Curl Up Press, 2018)*

Notes

1. What's Your Why?

1. Wagner-Stafford, Boni. *One Million Readers: The Definitive Guide to a Nonfiction Book Marketing Strategy That Saves Time, Money, and Sells More Books.* (Toronto, Canada: Ingenium Books Publishing Inc. 1st edition 2018, 2nd edition 2020)

2. What's Holding You Back?

1. Epstein, Joseph. "Think You Have a Book in You? Think Again." *New York Times,* September 28, 2002. https://web.archive.org/web/20201217214629/https://www.nytimes.com/2002/09/28/opinion/think-you-have-a-book-in-you-think-again.html
2. Smith, D., Schlaepfer, P., Major, K. *et al.* Cooperation and the evolution of hunter-gatherer storytelling. *Nature Communications* **8,** 1853 (2017). https://doi.org/10.1038/s41467-017-02036-8

3. What is Memoir

1. *Online Etymology Dictionary.* https://web.archive.org/web/20201218131901/https://www.etymonline.com/word/fiction
2. *Online Etymology Dictionary.*

4. Your Reader and Why They Buy

1. Wagner-Stafford. *One Million Readers.*
2. Edwards, Jim. *Copywriting Secrets: How Everyone Can Use The Power Of Words To Get More Clicks, Sales and Profits . . . No Matter What You Sell Or Who You Sell It To!* (Author Academy Elite, 2019)

5. Copyright

1. "A Brief History of Copyright," Intellectual Property Rights Office. https://web.archive.org/web/20200921013709/https://www.iprightsoffice.org/copyright_history/

2. "Copyright Certificate Graduates," Copyright Laws. https://web.archive.org/web/20201118173418/https://www.copyrightlaws.com/copyright-certificate-graduates/#cccl

3. "The International Copyright Symbol," Copyright Laws. https://web.archive.org/web/20201218132542/https://www.copyrightlaws.com/copyright-symbol-notice-year/

4. "Copyright," Canadian Intellectual Property Office. https://web.archive.org/web/20201218132733/http://www.ic.gc.ca/eic/site/cipointernet-internetopic.nsf/eng/h_wr00003.html

5. "Summary of the Berne Convention for the Protection of Literary and Artistic Works (1886)," World Intellectual Property Organization. https://web.archive.org/web/20201218132827/https://www.wipo.int/treaties/en/ip/berne/summary_berne.html

6. Fair Dealing Week. https://web.archive.org/web/20200228174008/https://www.uleth.ca/lib/copyright/content/fair_dealing_week/fair_dealing_vs_fair_use.asp

7. Wagner-Stafford, Boni. "Indie Authors & U.S. Copyright Law," Ingenium Books blog. Ingenium Books Publishing Inc. https://web.archive.org/web/20201218133057/https://ingeniumbooks.com/6-things-about-u-s-copyright-law-indie-authors-today/

8. Wagner-Stafford, Boni. "Six Things I Bet You Didn't Know About Canadian Copyright Law," Ingenium Books blog, Ingenium Books Publishing Inc. https://web.archive.org/web/20201218133224/https://ingeniumbooks.com/everything-you-wanted-to-know-about-canadian-copyright-law-but-were-afraid-to-ask/

9. Wagner-Stafford, Boni. "UK Copyright Law for Indie Authors," Ingenium Books blog, Ingenium Books Publishing, Inc. https://web.archive.org/web/20201218133410/https://ingeniumbooks.com/uk-copyright-law/

10. Wagner-Stafford, Boni. "Nine Essential Elements of Copyright Law in Australia," Ingenium Books blog, Ingenium Books Publishing Inc. https://web.archive.org/web/20201218133519/https://ingeniumbooks.com/nine-essential-elements-copyright-law-in-australia/

9. Draft Your Outline

1. Newell, John. *Let It Out: Train your voice to be free, free your voice to be trained.* Vancouver, Canada. John Newell 2013 https://ingeniumbooks.com/liojn

2. Newell, John. "Before You Write, Get All Your Ideas Out," Ingenium Books blog, Ingenium Books Publishing Inc. https://web.archive.org/web/20201218133750/https://ingeniumbooks.com/before-you-write-your-book-get-all-your-ideas-out/

3. "Hero's Journey 101: Definition and Step-by-Step Guide," Reedsy blog, Reedsy. https://web.archive.org/web/20201218133916/https://blog.reedsy.com/heros-journey/

11. Self-Awareness, Pain, Vulnerability

1. Gordon, Chad. "The Importance of Self-Awareness with Tasha Eurich," Blanchard Leader Chat (podcast), a Forum to Discuss Leadership and Management Issues, https://web.archive.org/web/20201218161307/https://leaderchat.org/2019/02/01/the-importance-of-self-awareness-with-tasha-eurich/#:~:text=%E2%80%9COur%20data%20reveals%20that%2095,%2Dawareness%3A%20internal%20and%20external Accessed November 25, 2020.

12. Libel, Slander, and Defamation

1. Sharpe, Michele. "Writing Memoir: Libel and Slander," Medium. https://web.archive.org/web/20201218162104/https://medium.com/@michelejsharpe/writing-memoir-libel-and-slander-ad30c188c0cf
2. Sember, Brette. "Differences Between Libel, Slander, and Defamation." Legalzoom. https://web.archive.org/web/20201218162339/https://www.legalzoom.com/articles/differences-between-defamation-slander-and-libel
3. Klar, Lewis N. "Defamation in Canada." The Canadian Encyclopedia. Retrieved from https://web.archive.org/web/20201218162455/https://www.thecanadianencyclopedia.ca/en/article/defamation

18. When to Choose Passive Voice

1. Bohner, Gerd. "Writing about rape: Use of the passive voice and other distancing text features as an expression of perceived responsibility of the victim," British Journal of Social Psychology (2001), 40, 515–529 Printed in Great Britain 2001. https://web.archive.org/web/20201218162834/https://www.researchgate.net/profile/Gerd_Bohner/publication/11563848_Writing_about_rape_Use_of_the_passive_voice_and_other_distancing_text_features_as_an_expression_of_perceived_responsibility_of_the_victim/links/5d4aa01ea6fdcc370a80f93a/Writing-about-rape-Use-of-the-passive-voice-and-other-distancing-text-features-as-an-expression-of-perceived-responsibility-of-the-victim.pdf
2. Phanichayakarn, Pera. "The effect of passive voice on perceived responsibility of the perpetrator," Master's thesis, Pacific University. (2013). Retrieved from:.https://web.archive.org/web/20201218163035/https://commons.pacificu.edu/work/sc/6b76a46d-7a36-45bb-a279-512daf792d95

19. What's Your English?

1. Abadi, Mark. "'Soda,' 'pop,' or 'coke': More than 400,000 Americans weighed in, and a map of their answers is exactly what you'd expect," Business Insider

(article) Oct 6, 2018, https://www.businessinsider.com/soda-pop-coke-map-2018-10?r=DE&IR=T

Other Books by Boni Wagner-Stafford

One Million Readers: The Definitive Guide to a Nonfiction Book Marketing Strategy That Saves Time, Money, and Sells More Books. (1st edition, Toronto, Canada, Ingenium Books Publishing Inc., 2019.)

Rock Your Business: 26 Essential Lessons to Start, Run, and Grow Your New Business from the Ground Up, with co-author John Wagner-Stafford. (Toronto, Canada. Ingenium Books Publishing Inc., 2019.)

contributing author and/or editor

Kitty Karma: Big Stories of the Small Cats Who Change Our Lives, Wai-Lin Terry. (Toronto, Canada. Kitty Karma Books, 2017.)

Wanted: How to Create a Relationship that Really Works, L.S. Clucas. (2nd edition, Cape Town, South Africa, L.S. Clucas)

other author coaching memoir work

My Fat Pants Don't Fit: A Mostly True Story of Divorce, Weight Loss, and Finally Finding Self-Love, Dina Marie. (Toronto, Canada. Ingenium Books Publishing Inc., 2020)

Four Fridays with Christina: Friendship, Death, and Lessons Learned by Letting Go Cynthia Barlow. (Toronto, Canada. Ingenium Books Publishing Inc., 2020)

The Picture Wall: One Woman's Story of Being His Her Their Mother, C.A. Gibbs. (Toronto, Canada. Ingenium Books Publishing Inc., 2020)

Flying With Dad: A Daughter. A Father. And the Hidden Gifts in His Stories from World War II, Yvonne Caputo. (Toronto, Canada. Ingenium Books Publishing Inc., 2020)

also published by Ingenium Books

Achieving Change: A Practical Guide for Creating Online Courses for Workplace Learning, Henrik J. Mondrup. (Toronto, Canada. Ingenium Books Publishing Inc., 2020)

In the Thick of It: Mastering the Art of Leading from the Middle, Gwyn Teatro. (2nd edition, Toronto, Canada. Ingenium Books Publishing Inc., 2020)

Just Do You: Leadership, Authenticity, and Your Personal Brand, Lisa King. (Toronto, Canada, Ingenium Books Publishing Inc., 2019)

Food, Mood, & Gratitude Journal: Learn to Take Charge of Your Health & Feel Great, Heidi Hackler. (Toronto, Canada. Ingenium Books Publishing Inc., 2019)

Prescription Technology: Opening Physician-Patient Communication Channels, Dr. Pranathi Kondapaneni. (Toronto, Canada. Ingenium Books Publishing Inc., 2019)

author development work

Unleash Culture, Discover Greatness Within. David Reeve. (Norsemen Books, 2016)

House Rich Cash Poor No More, No More: How to use the equity in your home to achieve financial freedom, David Rhodd. (Toronto, Canada. Ingenium Books Publishing Inc., 2018)

HELP! This Meeting Sucks: How to fix bad meetings and reignite people and performance, Peg Drummond. (Norsemen Books, 2018)

Recalculating: Find Financial Success and Never Feel Lost Again, Darren Coleman. (Norsemen Books, 2016)

Printed in Great Britain
by Amazon